We've Lost.
What Now?

We've Lost.
What Now?

Practical Counsel from the Book of Daniel

Wayne Baxter

Foreword by
Lee Beach

WIPF & STOCK · Eugene, Oregon

WE'VE LOST. WHAT NOW?
Practical Counsel from the Book of Daniel

Copyright © 2015 Wayne Baxter. All rights reserved. Except for brief quotations in critical publications or reviews, no part of this book may be reproduced in any manner without prior written permission from the publisher. Write: Permissions, Wipf and Stock Publishers, 199 W. 8th Ave., Suite 3, Eugene, OR 97401.

Wipf & Stock
An Imprint of Wipf and Stock Publishers
199 W. 8th Ave., Suite 3
Eugene, OR 97401

www.wipfandstock.com

ISBN 13: 978-1-62564-776-4

Manufactured in the U.S.A.

Henry Bosch, Our Daily Bread®, © 1984 by RBC Ministries, Grand Rapids, MI. Reprinted by permission. All rights reserved.

Scripture quotations marked (NIV) are taken from the Holy Bible, New International Version®, NIV®. Copyright © 1973, 1978, 1984 by Biblica, Inc.™ Used by permission of Zondervan. All rights reserved worldwide.

To Lu, my remarkable wife, and to our three amazing sons, Ethan, Micah, and Jared

Contents

Acknowledgments | ix
Foreword by Lee Beach | xi
Preface | xv

Introduction | 1

Part 1: Daniel's Witness to His Community

1. Experiencing God's Presence | 11
2. Walking in Humility | 22
3. Showing Commitment | 31
4. Genuinely Caring | 41
5. Engaging with Excellence | 51
6. Embracing Integrity | 62

Part 2: God's Message for His Community

7. God Is Infinitely Great | 75
8. God's Timing Is Always Perfect | 90
9. Pray Wisely | 97
10. Pray Alertly | 109
11. There's Hope for the Persecuted | 117

Conclusion | 134

Bibliography | 141

Acknowledgments

THERE ARE A NUMBER of people I wish to thank for their invaluable assistance in this writing project. I would like to thank my friend and former C & MA colleague, Dr. Lee Beach, Assistant Professor of Christian Ministry at McMaster Divinity College. Because Lee's own academic interest lies in the area of the church in postmodernity, he provided an excellent first set of critical eyes. His detailed comments and specific criticisms made this book far, far better than it would have been otherwise. I would like to thank two of my Heritage Seminary colleagues, Drs. Gord Oeste and Stan Fowler, for reviewing the early chapters. I am profoundly grateful to my amazing wife, Lucille. I wrote the first draft of this book years ago, while studying for my comprehensive exams during the second year of my doctoral program at McMaster University. Those were good days but busy—sometimes a tad chaotic. Lu served our young family well! Finally, I remain a deeply thankful debtor to my Lord Jesus Christ, who long ago imparted the vision for this book, as well as the grace to see it through to completion in his good time.

Foreword

Anyone paying even the slightest amount of attention to contemporary North American culture knows that we are living in a time of incalculable change. Perhaps the only constant left in North American life is the reality of perpetual change. Whether it is the changing landscape of gender roles, family constructs, career expectations, sexual mores, leisure activities, or technology, the one sure thing is that things do not stop changing. Of course, this reality also stretches into the world of religion.

Ever since the middle of the twentieth century the place of the church in Western society has undergone a seismic shift. After centuries of living at or near the center of Western culture, the church has slowly, or maybe not so slowly, found itself being moved from its place as a central institution in and shaper of Western culture. The church has moved from a place of cultural power to the fringes of Western society. This relocation is not something that demands much debate. It has become the undeniable social reality for Christians living in most parts of North America, and it will become the reality for those who still find themselves in cultural enclaves where the change has not yet been quite so pronounced. The reality of this shift means that it is time to move past questions about "Why this has happened?" or "How can we reverse the trend?" to "How should the church respond to its new cultural location?" and "What does it mean to be a people on the margins as opposed to a people at the center?"

In response to these questions there are a number of voices (dare I say an increasing number) that would assert that the best way to understand the church's move to the margins is through the paradigm of exile. This idea suggests that the concept of exile is one that addresses the experience of being moved from a place of influence and cultural predominance to one of marginalization. It can be argued that this kind of social dislocation is akin to the experience of being exiled.

Exile is not simply about being cast out of one's own land and being forced to live in another country, hoping that perhaps one day a return to the homeland will occur. Rather, exile means "living away from home," in all of the multifaceted ways that such an experience entails. Exile happens when we experience the reality of discovering that the place that once felt like home no longer feels like home. It happens when we find that our experience of a particular place has changed so much that we find ourselves no longer on the inside looking out, but rather on the outside looking in. Exile involves feeling displaced, even if the geographic locale has not changed. This is the experience of many Western Christians. Not long ago in Western culture there was at least a loose cultural consensus that largely privileged, affirmed, or at least respected the values and beliefs of a Christian worldview. This is no longer the case. The culture in which the church finds itself today has changed; it no longer feels the same. It is increasingly far from "home."

This kind of experience has its benefits for the contemporary church, not the least of which is that it puts us back in touch with the exilic experience of our ancestors in the faith, ancient Israel. As a nation Israel understood what it was to be a people whose religion held a privileged place in its culture. However, they also knew what it meant to lose that position and become a people on the margins. When exiled to Babylonia their question became the same that we now have to ask: "What does it mean to be a people on the margins as opposed to a people at the center?" One of the answers to that question is the book of Daniel. The story of Daniel teaches a marginalized people how to address the realities of life in the midst of cultural exile. The story casts a hopeful vision for how Israel, as God's people could thrive in exile. The Book of Daniel, as Wayne Baxter wonderfully demonstrates, can be equally as helpful for the church today.

What the church needs today is both a theological vision for who it is as a people in this time of complex change and some practical guidance for what it means to live out its faith under these new circumstances. Baxter provides the reader with both of these in his practical exegesis of Daniel's story. He works explicitly with the motif of exile as a primary way for the church to identify itself today, however, he avoids any hopelessness that such a paradigm could bring by consistently pointing the reader to the hopeful vision that Daniel offers for the possibility of cultural engagement

Foreword

and exilic mission. Further, he works closely with the real issues that Daniel deals with. In the chapters of this book you will find thoughtful reflection on: the way that Daniel wrestled with the presence of God in the midst of challenging circumstances, how Daniel approached working with people in power when he himself had little, the kind of character that is needed to engage society from the margins, and the character of God that remains constant even when our circumstances do not.

As a book written to address the needs of a community trying to maintain and even advance their faith, Daniel was never intended to be some esoteric theological treatise that was only loosely engaged with the realities of life in this world. It was a text of "practical theology" given to the Jewish people as a guide to life "away from home." Baxter is true to that same spirit in this volume as he offers a depth of teaching that never loses sight of the need for Daniel to speak relevantly to the needs of the church today. This is never truer than in the second half of the book, when Dr. Baxter tackles the apocalyptic visions of Daniel 7–12, which have often been far less accessible to the average reader than the stories of the first six chapters. The reader will benefit from the approach used in these chapters.

Like any book worth its salt there may be places where you will disagree with the author's position or conclusions. At times Baxter may make you bristle a bit with the challenges that he presents to contemporary Christians in this volume. However, bear in mind that it is likely that the book of Daniel itself probably made some members of its original audience bristle. Such is the nature of the biblical text that is under consideration here.

Most importantly, this book calls the church to remain focused on its mission to the world. Daniel ultimately is a book that reminds ancient Jews that by living out their commitment to God in a wise way they could influence those they lived amongst to become worshipers of Yahweh. This is a reminder that the people of God constantly need. Chapter 7 of this book recalls another biblical figure, Jonah, and his reluctance to engage in God's mission as being representative of both Israel and the church. Exile can make us long for the "good old days," or to "batten down the hatches" and try to weather the storm, all the while keeping our distance from the complex realities of the world around us. Neither of these options reflects faithfulness to the God of mission. In this book Wayne Baxter challenges us to take our current context seriously and to engage it wisely as a people who have been called by God to be his missional people. There are few books in the Bible better than Daniel for speaking to the kind of reality the church

Foreword

in the West now faces. Wayne Baxter has done us a service by offering this lucid volume as a resource for helping us understand the applicability of Daniel to our day. If the church takes this kind of guidance seriously then there is a lot of reason to hope that, just as it was for ancient Israel, exile can be a time of making fresh connections with God and participating in his ongoing mission in new and even surprising ways.

Lee Beach
McMaster Divinity College
Hamilton, Ontario

Preface

THIS BOOK STEMS FROM my personal conviction that the Western church, and in particular the church in my native Canada, has been and continues to be in exile. By "exile" I do not mean horrific geopolitical exile, like the kind the nation of Israel suffered as described in the Scriptures. Rather, I am referring to one of the effects of geopolitical exile: social and cultural marginalization.

The church of the West has become a marginalized institution. In other words, the church and its teaching have been pushed or "exiled" from the epicentre of society, a position it long enjoyed in previous generations, to its very fringes. While there have been many consequences of this sociocultural displacement, I believe one of the most potent yet unrecognized results is a seismic shift in the landscape for Christian ministry. The church once ministered from a position of strength: it was a widely respected institution whose basic tenets were near givens for much of society. Now, however, having been shoved to the edges of society, the church ministers from a position of weakness characterized by society's ambivalence, distrust, and even open animosity toward it. If the church is to bear in this present day the abundant fruit that Christ desires, then it needs to learn to minister from this position or status of exile. I believe that the book of Daniel, whose narrative setting is exile, is especially tailored for a socially and culturally exilic church, and therefore offers important lessons for bearing fruit in exile. The purpose of my book is to explore some of these lessons.

With that said, I need to issue a few disclaimers. First of all, unlike many popular books on Daniel, mine is not a book on "Christian prophecy," seeking to cull the soil of Daniel for hidden secrets to unlock the time in which we now live. These kinds of books tend to be more sensational than exegetically sensible. They also tend to be narcissistic by elevating the

Preface

modern reader above the original audience—as if the text was meant more for us than them. Neither is my book meant to be a rigorous academic commentary on the book of Daniel. There are many large and significant historical, social, theological, and literary questions surrounding the book of Daniel, and as a member of the academic guild, I believe that these questions are well worth discussing—just not here. Since the focus of this book is on how Daniel lived his life, these larger sorts of questions are ignored. Further, because this book concentrates on the theme of Daniel's witness to his community, I have been somewhat selective in my approach to Daniel: I do not deal with every single verse but only those that advance the theme of Daniel's exilic message.

Although I have translated Daniel from the original Hebrew and Aramaic for a doctoral seminar I took as a PhD student, I have chosen to cite from the NIV because of its continued widespread familiarity among Bible readers. While it's always best to read books like this one with your Bible open, I recognize that this is not always possible. So, rather than simply giving Bible references, I quote fairly extensively from Daniel, as well as from other parts of the Bible.

The chapter division of my book follows that of Daniel (in the English, which is slightly different than the Hebrew/Aramaic of the Masoretic Text), with the exception of my final chapter, which combines Daniel 11 and 12. And like Daniel, my book is subdivided into two parts: the first six chapters deal with the kind of lifestyle Daniel lived before his community and the message it sent; the second section deals with the series of visions that God gave him both to fuel his witness and to encourage his people during their period of exile. At the end of each chapter I have included some questions that I hope will foster deep, personal, communal, and practical reflection on a few of the essential points discussed in each chapter in order to help Christians live out their faith more effectively.

May Jesus Christ be praised!

Wayne Baxter
Heritage College and Seminary
Cambridge, Ontario

Introduction

OVER THE LAST DECADE or so it seems as if God has made a bit of a comeback. It has become commonplace to hear sports, music, and film celebrities refer to God positively. Regularly they "thank God" or "give praise to Jesus" after winning an award or accomplishing some great feat. I suspect that many of these entertainers invoke the name of God or Jesus either out of superstition (perhaps in an attempt to ensure continued success) or because it's simply the way they were raised. I am also sure that there are some genuine believers who do it because they are sincerely trying to witness to the watching public. But, is all witnessing *wise witnessing*?

During "hype week" of the 2002 Super Bowl, in which the St. Louis Rams played the New England Patriots, I listened with interest to a number of devout St. Louis Rams players routinely witness for Christ during their press conferences. They spoke often of how God had led them to the Super Bowl, how they felt God was now with them and therefore they believed they were a team of destiny. They spoke very specifically and very candidly about Christ being a part of their lives and a part of the game. I read a couple of noted sports columnists' opinions of what these devout Christians were saying, and their views were identical. They angrily and sarcastically wondered how a person of faith could believe that God was more concerned about who won a football game than he would be about the poor in Africa or the oppressed in Asia or the homeless in America. I found myself agreeing with these columnists because that was the clear inference of what these Christian athletes were saying. They probably didn't mean it that way, but that's precisely how it came across. Again I ask: is all witnessing *wise witnessing*?

WE'VE LOST. WHAT NOW?

Seeing the Landscape Clearly

If these athletes had said these things in a church setting of some kind—like a worship service or a fellowship gathering—then I would answer yes: they gave a wise witness. If they had said them a generation or two ago, I would have responded the same way. Why? Because that was back in an era when the Judeo-Christian heritage was a central part of the fabric of our society. That was when "Christendom" still flourished in North America.

Christendom began in the fourth century under Roman Emperor Constantine. While Christianity had started out as a tiny, feeble, and ostracized movement, under Constantine it became the official religion of the Roman Empire, and thus enjoyed newfound state powers and privileges like no other. By the Middle Ages the church and state had become thoroughly intertwined: state churches were the order of the day, and in some countries the king or queen automatically became the head of the church. During the height of Christendom, members of society were assumed to be Christian by virtue of birth rather than by choice. Christianity was very much part of the culture of the West, or as Craig Van Gelder, Professor of Domestic Missiology at Calvin Theological Seminary, put it: Western society was a "churched culture."[1] It could be safely assumed that a person from the West believed, at least at some level, in the Judeo-Christian God and possessed a basic familiarity with the Bible and Christian teaching.

That's why I said that if the Rams players had said these things a couple of generations ago they would have witnessed wisely: most people would have been onside with what they were saying. But their forum that week was neither the church nor the friendly confines of Christendom. Their audience was the twenty-first-century marketplace, and the Judeo-Christian principles upon which the US and Canada were founded have increasingly vanished from public purview in the US, and have been all but replaced by secular pluralism in Canada.

Other commentators have made similar observations about our cultural landscape. In a recent *National Post* column, Rex Murphy recalls how, back in the 1950s, it was quite "natural" for people to think in Christian terms: "[H]ow astonished an ordinary person would be to hear an outsider ridicule the Trinity, or mock the Immaculate Conception, or any other of the mysteries of the ancient Catholic church—or any church to which they

---

1. Van Gelder, "Missional Challenge," 55.

Introduction

belonged."[2] But Murphy continues, "[H]ow great a shift there has been from the complacent, settled and confident adherence to religions and religious principles that was not so long ago the habit of most of the Western world."[3] In his book *Evangelism after Christendom*, Boston University professor Bryan Stone writes how evangelism today is especially problematic for Christians "in societies where Christianity has historically been tied to the center of political, economic, and cultural power but in which the old 'Christendom' model has for some time now been crumbling."[4] What have been the signs of the "crumbling" of Christendom?

Perhaps the most obvious crack in the foundation has been declining church attendance. Prominent University of Lethbridge sociologist Reginald Bibby has noted how weekly church attendance in Canada peeked in the 1950s: seven out of ten Canadians attended church on a weekly (yes, weekly!) basis.[5] In 2005 only 25 percent of Canadians attended church weekly.[6]

Deep fractures exist in our educational system. Many universities were founded for the expressed purpose of strengthening the church. In 1636 the founders of Harvard had clear motives for establishing the school. Their reasons remain permanently etched on a tablet on the Johnston Gate entrance to Harvard Yard:

> After God had carried us safe to New England and we had built our houses, provided necessaries for our livelihood, reared convenient places for God's worship, and settled the civil government: One of the next things we longed for and looked after was to advance learning and perpetuate it to posterity; *dreading to leave an illiterate ministry to the churches, when our present ministers shall lie in the dust.* (emphasis added)

Harvard, one of the world's most prestigious universities, was originally started to ensure that future church leaders would be highly educated and trained for ministry. Almost five hundred years later few would ever associate Harvard University with the training of local church pastors.

Likewise, numerous Canadian universities began with a similar ethos. The mottos of some academic institutions sound like something from a

---

2. Murphy, "Secularism."
3. Ibid.
4. Stone, *Christendom*, 10.
5. Bibby, *Restless Gods*, 20.
6. Project Canada Surveys Press Release.

We've Lost. What Now?

Puritan devotional: "Send forth thy light and thy truth" (Laurentian University); "Prayer and work" (Dalhousie University); "God is the Master of Science" (University of Ottawa); "All things cohere in Christ" (McMaster University). What I find ironic about McMaster's motto, taken from Colossians 1:17, is that the word "Christ" does not actually appear in the verse, but rather, "him": "[a]ll things cohere in him." Apparently, the framers of McMaster's motto wanted to remove any trace of ambiguity. Talk about putting "Christ" back into Christmas!

But things have changed drastically since then. As a former teaching assistant for McMaster's course on world religions, I was cautioned not to privilege one religion (Christianity) above the others. In a January 24, 2013, *National Post* commentary written in response to articles supporting Christian institution Trinity Western University's plan to open a law school, law professors representing the universities with the mottos "Prayer and work" and "God is the Master of Science" strongly opposed TWU, claiming, "No person can truly think critically from one pre-determined lens, in this case, a lens mandated by TWU." The crumbling of Christendom.

More evidence for this collapse can be witnessed by a shift in the basic presuppositions of our society. Imagine sitting on a park bench, enjoying the warmth and the sun on a clear, beautiful summer day. You are joined by someone who sits next to you. You begin to chat. Wanting to witness to this person, you casually mention your amazement of creation and "God." A generation or two ago, before the crumbling of Christendom, the person next to you would almost certainly have assumed that you were talking about the Judeo-Christian God. And surely, you would have assumed that they would assume that. Today, however, in our secular pluralistic society such an assumption would be naïve: "God" could mean the Judeo-Christian God, but it could also mean Allah, Brahman, Buddha, some unknown cosmic god, or something else.

There was a time when rudimentary Bible knowledge was a given. I remember as a kid watching sporting events on TV and seeing the John 3:16 guy: the bespectacled, multicolored-afro-sporting man who would hold up a large placard that read "John 3:16." Now obviously, most people who read that sign didn't know exactly what John 3:16 said, but I'm also pretty sure that almost everybody knew at least that "John 3:16" was a Bible verse. But that was then. . . .

Former *Tonight Show* host Jay Leno had a segment called "Jaywalking" in which he asked unsuspecting people on the street some questions

Introduction

about current events or topics of public interest, showcasing some of the more outrageously wrong answers. A few times he quizzed people on basic Bible knowledge. The results were both hilarious and sad. Jay asked one Las Vegas bartender how long ago he thought Jesus was born. The man sheepishly answered, "Oh, about four hundred years ago." Jay straight-facedly responded, "So, about the same time Columbus came over," to which the man embarrassingly replies, "I was so wrong." Hmm, you think?

A number of years ago I encountered this firsthand while teaching a New Testament survey course at a major Canadian university. I had my students take a multiple choice test on basic New Testament facts as a way for me to gauge their knowledge of the subject because I didn't want to teach over their heads or beneath them. The questions were the epitome of basic: "How many Gospels are there in the New Testament?"; "How many apostles did Jesus appoint?"; and so forth. In a class of almost eighty students, half failed and a quarter barely passed. Seminary professor, author, and blogger Brandon Withrow testifies of similar results, noting at his own school that there are "a growing number of students who enter a seminary education with very little background knowledge of their own religion. Basic teachings of the faith and major historical figures are not even on the radar for many students."[7] . . . This is now.

Back to the 2002 St. Louis Rams. Were those Rams players witnessing wisely? I would have to answer no. I believe they were sincere, but they were not wise—as evidenced by the specific charge voiced by those two sports columnists. Christendom has crumbled away. On the one hand, there has been a seismic shift in the presuppositions, values, and culture of our society that necessarily affects how spiritual things are understood. So, seated on that park bench on a bright, sunny day, you begin to share with the person sitting next to you, "God loves you and has a wonderful plan for your life." The person smiles and nods in agreement, and so you continue. However, you assume that she thinks you're referring to the Judeo-Christian God, when in fact she's on a completely different set of theological tracks. In the end, she prays the "Sinner's Prayer," but did she really understand God, Jesus, and the gospel in a salvific way, or has she simply added, rather than substituted, Jesus and the gospel to her system of beliefs and practices? The colossal shift in presuppositions makes communicating the gospel—at the basic level of understanding—much more difficult than ever before.

---

7. Withrow, "Religious Literacy Survey."

On the other hand, not only is the church no longer held in high regard, but in some (increasingly larger) circles of our society it is despised. In the eyes of many, its "best before" date has long since passed. That is why, for example, there was so much negative hoopla surrounding former NFL player Tim Tebow. Pundits frequently described him as a deeply "polarizing" figure. If Tebow was polarizing, I don't believe it was necessarily because of what he said, although to be honest I do believe this played a role (I'll return to this point later, in the Conclusion). It was certainly not how he said what he said: his tone was always humble, gracious, and charitable. Rather, I think it was *where* he was saying what he was saying: the marketplace, whose complexion has, as I've been arguing, changed drastically in the last couple of generations. Frankly, I just don't think "Tebow Time" would have caused such a kerfuffle in the era preceding the rupturing of Christendom's fault lines. But secular pluralism has gradually exiled the church to the periphery of society, and it is from this position of marginalization that the church collectively and Christians individually must learn once again how to minister effectively.

Receiving Help from a Faithful Friend

It has been said many times that the Bible is the Christian's handbook for faith and practice. While that is true, are there sections of it that are especially applicable at certain times? I think the book of Daniel speaks very specifically to the church collectively and to Christians individually because it describes a parallel situation. If there was such a thing as Christendom, then I think that in the metanarrative of the Bible there was something that I would call "Jewishdom."

Jewishdom would have begun to emerge after the conquest, when, led by Joshua and his successors, Israel drove out most of the nations that had previously inhabited Palestine. Jewishdom would have been at its strongest during the time of the monarchy. If we focus on the southern kingdom of Judah (since that is where Daniel comes from), then from the time of the conquest to the Babylonian exile spans about eight hundred years (although dating with exact precision is always tricky). That means for eight centuries Judaism was at the epicenter of Palestinian culture and society. The biblical vision for Jewish society, featuring the centrality of Yahweh as the one true God, was assumed by many if not most. If someone turned to the person next to them on that park bench and talked about "God," s/he

Introduction

would have been referring to Yahweh. Temple attendance would have been presupposed in most places, and the Hebrew Bible (i.e., the Christian Old Testament) would have been widely known, believed, taught, and followed to varying degrees. Judaism was the hub of Palestinian society. But that all changed after the Babylonian exile and the destruction of Jerusalem.

The exile forcefully pushed the Jews to the margins of society geopolitically. Many Jews like Daniel were taken away from their homeland to live in a foreign land. Moreover, for these Jews the religious, cultural, and social landscape in which they had grown up instantly transformed into something dramatically different: not only was Yahweh not the only God, he wasn't even the mightiest one; it was kind of hard to go to the temple given that the Babylonians had leveled it; the vast majority of the Jews' Babylonian neighbors knew absolutely nothing about the Bible or its teachings. Judaism had become simply one of the many different religions in the Babylonian Empire. In short, the exile marked the collapse of "Jewishdom."

That's the basic background to Daniel's story. Daniel, then, is emblematic of believers today in exile, living in the margins of society. I believe the story of Daniel can help the church corporately and Christians individually become more fruitful in exile. Daniel offers us some very specific ways that we can learn afresh how to witness wisely in our society and thus minister more effectively from the margins. And it is to these lessons we now turn.

Part 1

Daniel's Witness to His Community

1

Experiencing God's Presence

If your Presence does not go with us, do not send us up from here. How will anyone know that you are pleased with me and with your people unless you go with us? What else will distinguish me and your people from all the other people on the face of the earth?

—EXOD 33:15-16

WHILE THE TERM "WAR hero" typically conjures up mental pictures of men, many were women; one of them being Mary Roberts Wilson. Wilson, who served as chief OR nurse in several different divisions of the Fifth Army during World War II, was the first woman to earn a Silver Star for courage under fire. She landed at Anzio Beach in southern Italy five days after the Allied invasion. At one point the fighting become so fierce that German shrapnel ripped through the operating tent as Wilson assisted in surgery. Consequently, her unit made arrangements for its fifty nursing staff to leave. Mary, however, refused to go. She reflected on the episode years later: "How could I possibly leave them? I was part of them." Because Mary Wilson felt deeply connected to the soldiers of her unit, she could not tear herself away from them, despite the intense danger. She would neither leave them nor forsake them.

The book of Daniel opens with a familiar formula: "In the third year of the reign of Jehoiakim king of Judah" (v. 1a). Daniel's original audience would have encountered this formula (viz., "In such and such year of the reign of so and so, king of Judah/Israel") frequently in the Scriptures: it appears more than sixty times in the books of Kings and Chronicles alone. The big difference in Daniel, however, is what immediately follows it: "Nebuchadnezzar king of Babylon came to Jerusalem and besieged it" (v. 1b). In the more militaristic sections of the Old Testament (like the books from Joshua to Chronicles) we often read of how God would "give" the enemy "into the hands" of his people. For example, when the king of Aram threatened to destroy Israel, the Lord said to King Ahab, "Do you see this vast [Aramean] army? I will give it into your hand today" (1 Kgs 20:13). Here in Daniel, however, the reverse is true: "[T]he Lord delivered"—literally, "gave"—"Jehoiakim king of Judah into his [i.e., Nebuchadnezzar's] hand" (v. 2a). God did not give the Babylonians into Israel's hand; he gave his people (represented by King Jehoiakim) into their enemy's hands. He sent them into exile.

To delve into all of the reasons for the Babylonian exile would take us too far afield. For our purposes here, we need only recall how the author of Kings viewed this disastrous turn of events:

> Surely these things happened to Judah according to the LORD'S command, in order to remove them from his presence because of the sins of Manasseh and all he had done. . . . For he had filled Jerusalem with innocent blood and the LORD was not willing to forgive. (2 Kgs 24:3–4)

Because the sins of Judah had reached an all-time high, the Lord felt compelled to send his people away from the Promised Land.

The setting of the story of Daniel, then, is exile. As utterly horrible as the Babylonian exile was physically, with its devastating carnage and national destruction, there was another central dimension to it. In his book *Cadences of Home*, Old Testament scholar Walter Brueggemann summarizes it like this:

> [T]he exiles experienced a loss of the structured, reliable world which gave them meaning and coherence, and they found themselves in a context where their most treasured and trusted symbols of faith were mocked, trivialized, or dismissed. Exile is not primally geographical, but it is social, moral, and cultural.[1]

Daniel's life is a story about living in social, moral, religious, and cultural exile. How should a believer live in such conditions?

---

1. Brueggemann, *Cadences*, 4.

Experiencing God's Presence

One of the crucial issues for Jews living in exile (i.e., Diaspora Jews, those living outside of the land of Palestine) was the presence of God: was God still with them? Israel knew that God would always be with them in the Land. For example, after King Solomon built the temple in Jerusalem, God filled it with his presence (1 Kgs 8:10–11). Consequently, a recurring motif in Solomon's prayer for the dedication of the temple is God's presence with the temple:

> May your eyes be open *toward this temple* night and day, *this place of which you said*, "*My Name shall be there*," so that you will hear the prayer your servant prays *towards this place*. Hear the supplication of your servant and of your people Israel when they pray *toward this place*. (1 Kgs 8:29–30, emphasis added; see also vv. 33, 35, 38, 42–44, 48).

In fact, it was because of this steadfast conviction of God's abiding presence with his people in the Land that some of the religious leaders in Jeremiah's day presumptuously believed that as long as the temple stood God would protect them from their enemies, no matter how morally irresponsibly they lived (see Jer 7:1–14).

That God would be with his people in the Land no pious Jew would ever have doubted. But what about outside the Land? The answer seems less clear. A few texts suggest a negative response. Solomon's prayer of dedication for the temple seems to imply that petitioners would only be heard if they physically oriented themselves toward the Jerusalem temple, where God's Name dwells: nine times in his prayer Solomon speaks of praying "towards the temple" or "towards Jerusalem." The book of Esther, which deals with Diaspora Jews, gained a measure of notoriety because the name of God is conspicuously missing from the story. During the canonization of the Jewish Scriptures, this "absence" of God led some Jews to deny Esther's divine inspiration and canonicity. Similarly, some Bible commentators today believe that this significant omission supports the contention that the story should be understood more critically: while God could still hear and act on behalf of his people living outside the Land, he was no longer with Diaspora Jews in the special way that he was with Jews in the Land.

Daniel had become a Diaspora Jew. Was God, then, still with Daniel? Or in other words, could Daniel still count on God despite suffering in national exile? This question of God's presence is put to rest early in the story of Daniel: "Now God had caused the official [in charge of Daniel and the other exiles] to show favor and compassion to Daniel" (v. 9). The Hebrew word translated "favor" (*ḥesed*) refers to God's abiding love for his covenant people. For example, when God revealed himself to Moses on Mount Sinai, he proclaimed, "The LORD, the LORD, the compassionate and gracious God, slow to anger, abounding in love [*ḥesed*] and faithfulness, maintaining love [*ḥesed*] to thousands and forgiving wickedness" (Exod 34:6–7a). This abiding love that God shows his covenant people is intrinsic to God's very nature. According to this verse in Daniel, God chose to show his abiding love to Daniel *through* his Babylonian captor.

Commentators agree that this verse alludes to the story of Joseph in the book of Genesis. Although Joseph had been unjustly imprisoned, Genesis states, "But while Joseph was there in prison, the LORD was with him; he showed him kindness and granted him favor in the eyes of the prison warden" (Gen 39:20b–21). It was because God was with Joseph that he received favor from the warden. The same connection is implied in Daniel: it is precisely because God is with Daniel that he experiences favor from the chief official, who, consequently agrees to Daniel's dietary experiment (vv. 10–16).

That God's presence brings favor to others is seen elsewhere in the Scriptures. For example, after the Jerusalem temple had been reconstructed and Ezra came from Babylonia to help re-establish the Jews in the Land, the Bible says that "The king had granted [Ezra] everything he asked, for the hand of the LORD his God was on him" (Ezra 7:6). Similarly, after successfully petitioning King Artaxerxes' for permission to return to help rebuild Jerusalem along with a royal escort and supplies, Nehemiah stated, "And because the gracious hand of my God was upon me, the king granted my requests" (Neh 2:8b).

Favor with others demonstrates that God abides with his people in a special way. Without God's presence believers could never hope to survive let alone thrive in exile. Second Kings 24:3–4 makes it plain that the exile was God's judgment upon the Jews for their sinful rebellion. Yet even in judgment God remembered mercy. Despite sending his people away from the Promised Land, his presence continued to be with them, and he could still bring them favor in exile. I think the same holds true for the church today. I believe that the collapse of Christendom is God's judgment upon the Western church because of the massive arrogance, independence, and resulting immorality that Christians (leaders and laity alike) have deliberately walked in for decades. Given 2 Kings 24:3–4, should we have expected anything different? But as with Daniel, in judgment God remembers mercy.

Experiencing God's Presence

He has sent us away—thrusting us from the social, moral, and cultural heart of society to its outer edges—but he abides with us still. His presence gives us reassurance that he will take care of us in the face of our difficult circumstances. I believe that Jesus had envisioned this when he commissioned his disciples to make disciples of all nations, promising them, "[S]urely I am with you always, to the very end of the age" (Matt 28:20b).

During one period in my life, I was unemployed for a long time, and whenever I did manage to find a job it was only short-term. If you have ever been unemployed for a long time, you know how stressful it can be (especially when trying to support a family), and the longer you go without a job the more depressing and discouraging it can be. On one occasion I worked in an automotive factory for two weeks. During my first week there, an employee whom I had never met approached me and said, "You look like a good guy. If you ever need a job, call Skyline Landscaping. Tell them Big John sent you." He never asked me my name and I never saw him after that. He was a total stranger, whom I barely knew from a hole in the wall (albeit a rather massive, muscular hole in the wall), yet he was basically offering me, a guy he didn't know from Adam, a job. Just in case things didn't work out for me at the factory. Well, the next week "just in case" arrived and I was laid off. But my unemployment soon ceased: I left a voice message with Skyline Landscaping, telling them, of course, that Big John sent me. They returned my call immediately, asked me for an interview, and offered me the job. I believe that because God was with me he granted me favor with Big John. And that favor was God's way of saying, "Wayne, don't worry about working. I'm taking care of you; everything is going to be fine. Trust me." Even though it didn't always seem like he was there, this was God's way of reminding me, "I will never leave you nor forsake you." God's presence grants us favor.

His presence grants us something else. Not only was God with Daniel and his friends, he had uniquely gifted them to thrive in exile:

> To these four young men God gave knowledge and understanding of all kinds of literature and learning. And Daniel could understand visions and dreams of all kinds. . . . The king talked with them, and he found none equal to Daniel, Hananiah, Mishael, and Azariah; so they entered the king's service. In every matter of wisdom and understanding about which the king questioned them, he found them ten times better than all the magicians and enchanters in his whole kingdom. (vv. 17, 19–20)

God equips his people to thrive in exile. God's presence imparted to these four youth a remarkable giftedness that really made people sit up and take notice: the king "found them ten times better than all the magicians and enchanters in his whole kingdom" (v. 20b). And their giftedness extended into both the natural and supernatural realms.

In the natural realm they demonstrated an extremely high aptitude for learning (v. 4) and an extensive breadth of knowledge in the arts that impressed the king and his court. Christians often overlook the fact that our natural abilities and talents are every bit as much a gift (a "charisma") from God as those more "spiritual" gifts that the Apostle Paul describes in some of his letters. For example, while craftsmanship does not make Paul's gift lists, it is described as such in the Old Testament: the Lord had chosen and filled Bezalel the craftsman "with the Spirit of God, with wisdom, with understanding, with knowledge and with all kinds of skills—to make artistic designs for work in gold, silver, and bronze, to cut and set stones, to work in wood and to engage in all kinds of artistic crafts" (Exod 35:31–33). Bezalel's giftedness in artistic design and craftsmanship operated through the Holy Spirit.

Similarly, Moses told the Israelites before crossing the Jordan that, although they might think that their own strength and power will make them rich in the Promised Land, they must always "remember the LORD your God, for it is he who gives you the ability to produce wealth" (Deut 8:18). God does not limit his gifts to the supernatural realm. Speed, leaping ability, hand-eye coordination, an excellent sense of smell or taste—all are gifts that God sovereignly and graciously imparts to people. And when these gifts are diligently exercised they bring God glory, which is ultimately why we have them. God equips his people to thrive in exile.

Daniel's giftedness also extended into the supernatural realm: "And Daniel could understand visions and dreams of all kinds" (v. 17b). We are not explicitly told if Daniel's three friends possessed this kind of ability. It's possible that they did. After all, while the narrative only singled out Daniel for his resolution not to defile himself with the royal food and wine (in v. 8), vv. 12–16 make it clear that Daniel's friends had this same commitment. But since Daniel is the main figure of the story, it is his particular giftedness that is showcased for the reader in the ensuing chapters.

A paradoxical situation exists today: people do not want religion but they do want God. Often, when unbelievers peer through the windows of the church, they are repulsed by what they see: a group of people who talk a lot about God and about having a personal relationship with him, but who lack the power thereof. They see a bunch of people slavishly living by sets of rules, rites, and regulations, but who show little evidence of God truly living in them and with them. The church has been marginalized yet much of society still seeks for spiritual reality and vitality.

The Bible offers us diverse signs and expressions of this spiritual reality and vitality. Perhaps topping the list is a transformed life, whereby God touches the heart of a lost rebel, causing this person to change course and pursue Christ in a passionate, devoted, and sustained manner. Clearly, another indicator of spiritual vitality would be the fruit of Spirit, which Paul describes in Galatians 5:22–23a: "But the fruit of the Spirit is love, joy, peace, forbearance, kindness, goodness, faithfulness, gentleness and self-control." The Holy Spirit produces this fruit, in increasing measure, in the lives of individual Christians. He also produces his fruit corporately in the life of the local church.

Consonant with Daniel 1:17, another expression of spiritual reality and vitality are the more revelatory gifts. Certainly this is what Luke envisioned. According to Acts, on the Day of Pentecost, Peter explained the signs to the watching crowds:

> [T]his is what was spoken by the prophet Joel: "In the last days, God says, I will pour out my Spirit on all people. Your sons and daughters will prophesy, your young men will see visions, your old men will dream dreams. Even on my servants, both men and women, I will pour out my Spirit in those days, and they will prophesy." (Acts 2:16–18; cf. Joel 2:28–29)

God promised to speak to his people through dreams, visions, and the like. The sharing of these revelations with others is prophecy. What I find intriguing about the last part of this citation in Acts 2 is that Luke (or Peter) seems to insert the word "prophesy" a second time into the original text of Joel. In other words, according to both the Hebrew text and the Septuagint (i.e., the Greek Old Testament of the early Christians, translated from the Hebrew), Joel 2:29 ends only with "I will pour out my Spirit." But Luke appends to these words the phrase "and they will prophesy." For Luke, then, one of the hallmarks of Christian ministry is the ability to prophesy by God's Spirit. The activity of the Holy Spirit is a key motif in Luke and Acts. The special role of prophecy in the book of Revelation also suggests that John saw the importance of prophecy for the church during the end times.

God's abiding presence imparts this gift. In the case of Daniel, God's presence with him enabled him to serve in this way in exile.

I do not believe this gifting that God's presence imparts has ceased. As exilic Daniel could speak prophetically to his community, so also I believe that God's presence with his exilic people today enables us to speak prophetically to our communities, as a sign of God's reality and vitality. During one of the small group gatherings to which my wife and I once belonged years ago, one of our members was having a miserable week. He had been pretty badly beaten up verbally and emotionally at work. After he very painfully shared this with us, our small group leader John felt that we should surround Gerry, lay hands on him, and pray for him. As we stood praying over him, one word suddenly popped into my head: "Jedidiah." I thought, "Okay, Lord, what am I supposed to do with this?" No sooner than I had silently prayed that thought did John say, "Gerry, I believe that the Lord wants to give you a new name [i.e., a nickname] to encourage you." No way! That must be it. So I said, rather sheepishly, "Gerry, I think I know the name God has for you: "Jedidiah." I remember reading that "Jedidiah" was God's nickname for Solomon at birth, and it means "loved by the Lord" (2 Sam 12:24–25). When I shared this with Gerry, he broke down and wept tears of joy. He had felt like God had abandoned him that week, that he had forsaken him, and that he didn't care. In reality, the very opposite was true: Gerry was "loved by the Lord."

While prophecy is often expressed verbally and individually, I believe that it can also be expressed non-verbally and corporately. That is to say, I think that the church speaks prophetically whenever Christians live in genuine community with each other. Bryan Stone writes how "the church does not really need an evangelistic strategy. The church *is* the evangelistic strategy."[2] Similarly, I believe that, apart from spoken words, *when the church lives in genuine community it is being prophetic.* As believers lovingly commune with each other, their life together offers an unspoken but nonetheless prophetic word to a watching public. Jesus told his followers, "By this everyone will know that you are my disciples, if you love one another" (John 13:35).

King David was one of the first writers to connect this sense of community to God's presence: "How good and pleasant it is when God's people live together in unity! It is like precious oil poured on the head, running down on the beard, running down on Aaron's beard, down upon the collar

---

2. Stone, *Christendom*, 15 (emphasis original).

of his robe" (Ps 133:1–2). David compares the unity of the assembly with the anointing of God's Holy Spirit, symbolized in the Old Testament by the anointing oil that was poured over Aaron as God's high priest. I think the psalmist's picture suggests that God's presence and authentic community are very much interrelated: God's Spirit brings unity and oneness, while unity and oneness brings a greater sense of God's presence.

The groups, clubs, and teams of this world are predicated on exclusivism: you have to have enough money to join; you have to dress a certain way or drive the right kind of car; you need to know the right people; you must look the part or be good enough to join. When Paul writes, then, that Christ himself has made peace for us and has destroyed "the dividing wall of hostility" between us (Eph 2:14) such that there is now "neither Jew nor Gentile, neither slave nor free, nor is there male and female, for you are all one in Christ Jesus" (Gal 3:28), his claim is startling because it runs completely counter to the social exclusivism routinely practiced by the world. That is why when the church lives in genuine community it speaks prophetically to our world: it simultaneously rebukes the world for its sinful social exclusivism and discrimination, while at the same time it invites people to become a part of something the world can never ultimately provide: communal oneness, marked by loving acceptance and belonging. This prophetic word-clothed-in-deed offers God's light to those living in moral darkness (Matt 5:14–16).

Back to Daniel. It came as no surprise to God that Daniel would live his life in exile. God not only knew that—after all, his prophets had predicted the exile generations in advance—he imparted to Daniel unique gifts to ensure that he would not just survive but thrive in his difficult circumstances. The first chapter of the book of Daniel serves as the foundation for the rest of the story. God's presence abides with Daniel despite his nation's defeated, marginalized status in exile, and he has gifted him to witness effectively during this period. I believe the same holds true for the church today. God knew that the Western church would eventually lose its footing in society and be shoved to the periphery. And yet, God is still there for us. In the midst of the mockery and the animosity that we so often attract, we can still humbly turn to God with confidence, knowing that he has not excused himself from the scene. Though we sometimes feeling abandoned, he has not left us as orphans (Isa 49:15). Therefore, although we live in exile we should never live with a sense of despair over our circumstances, simply biding time until Jesus "calls it" and finally returns for his church. For not only can we count on God's abiding presence, he has also given us unique gifts to equip us in our exile in order to enable us to speak prophetically, through word and deed, to a watching world so that we can witness more effectively to our community.

God is with us. He has neither left us nor forsaken us, and he has designed us to thrive even in such a time as this.

Questions for Further Reflection

1. What are some signs that you have personally seen that the church is presently in social, moral, and cultural "exile"?

2. How have some churches reacted to their exilic environment? In other words, have they adjusted their ministries in some way, or have they simply stayed the course and continued along as if nothing has changed?

3. Have you ever felt abandoned by God? What kind of circumstances created this feeling?

Experiencing God's Presence

4. When struggling with feelings of abandonment, have there been some specific ways that God has shown you that he has not left you and still abides with you in order to take care of you?

5. Have there been times when God was trying to speak to you but you missed it? Describe one of these times. What are some steps you can take to help you not miss what God wants to say to you?

2

Walking in Humility

For all those who exalt themselves will be humbled, and those who humble themselves will be exalted.

—LUKE 14:11

A TRULY HUMBLE MAN IS hard to find, yet God delights to honor such selfless people. Booker T. Washington, the renowned eighteenth–nineteenth-century Black educator, was an outstanding example of this truth. Shortly after he took over the presidency of Tuskegee Institute in Alabama, he was walking in an exclusive section of town when he was stopped by a wealthy White woman. Not knowing the famous man by sight, she asked if he would like to earn a few dollars by chopping wood for her. Because he had no pressing business at that moment, Professor Washington smiled, rolled up his sleeves, and proceeded to do the humble chore she had requested. When he was finished, he carried the logs into the house and stacked them by the fireplace. A girl recognized him and later revealed his identity to the lady. The next morning the embarrassed woman went to see Washington in his office at the Institute and apologized profusely. "It's perfectly all right, Madam," he replied. "Occasionally I enjoy a little manual labor. Besides, it's always a delight to do something for a friend." She shook his hand warmly and assured him that his meek and gracious attitude had endeared him and his work to her heart. Not long afterward she showed her admiration by persuading some wealthy acquaintances to join her in donating thousands of dollars to Tuskegee Institute. "For all those who exalt themselves will be humbled, and those who humble themselves will be exalted."

According to our text in Daniel 2, even the most powerful rulers can lose sleep: "In the second year of his reign, Nebuchadnezzar had dreams; his mind was troubled and he could not sleep" (v. 1). What a pity: all that power, all that money, all those possessions, and the guy still couldn't buy a good night's sleep! What is a person to do? Well, the king had a plan. Sensing that this dream had a spiritual significance, and knowing that neither his power nor his money could help him understand his dream, he called on his wise men to help him (vv. 2–3). But there is only one problem—that is, as far as the wise men are concerned—the king didn't trust them:

> This is what I have firmly decided: If you do not tell me what my dream was and interpret it, I will have you cut into pieces and your houses turned into piles of rubble. But if you tell me the dream and explain it, you will receive from me gifts and rewards and great honor. So tell me the dream and interpret it for me. (vv. 5–6)

Nebuchadnezzar, knowing that dream interpretation can be very subjective and that a false interpretation can sound as plausible as a true one, shrewdly demanded that the interpreters state the content of his dream first. I cannot help but find this humorous: the king had hired this group of men to be his loyal advisors, yet he didn't even trust them. It's like the man who had been apprehensive about his first airplane ride. His friends, eager to hear how it went, asked if he enjoyed the flight. "Well," the man commented, "it wasn't as bad as I thought it might be, but I'll tell you this: I never did put all my weight down!" Neither did Nebuchadnezzar put all of the weight of his trust in his advisors.

I don't think we should be too hasty in thinking this was just a problem in Babylonia, though. Balaam was considered to be a prophet of the Lord, yet on occasion he could be bribed into giving false prophecies (Num 22:4–7a; 24:1). And in a rather curious biblical account, the prophet known only as the "man of God" fell victim to the false prophecy of the "old prophet living in Bethel" who, after scheming against the man of God, correctly prophesied his doom (1 Kgs 13:1–32). So I suppose where there's prophesy there's also false prophecy.

King Nebuchadnezzar's demand shocked his wise men:

> There is no one on earth who can do what the king asks! No king, however great and mighty, has ever asked such a thing of any magician or enchanter or astrologer. What the king asks is too

difficult. No one can reveal it to the king except the gods, and they do not live among humans. (vv. 10–11)

Nebuchadnezzar, however, firmly thought otherwise, and in a fit of fury ordered the execution of all his wise men, including Daniel and his three friends (vv. 12–13). When Daniel heard of this, he petitioned the king for time to interpret the dream. What strikes me the most about the ensuing narrative is the humility that Daniel displayed, both publicly and privately.

Publicly, Daniel humbled himself by asking Nebuchadnezzar for time. While Daniel had the ability to interpret dreams and visions, he recognized that *God-given ability does not operate independently of God but in dependence upon God.* That's why he asked the king for more time rather than trying to do it in his own power. Daniel needed time to seek God concerning the dream. When you have a gift or a talent it's easy to fall into the trap of thinking that you don't really need God in order to use it. After all, aren't my gifts at my disposal to use at my command? Well, in one respect, yes: God has endowed people with gifts and abilities (like drawing, singing, running, teaching, etc.) that can be spontaneously summoned in an almost flip-switch manner. Yet, more must be said. On the one hand, I would argue that, while our gifts might function without any conscious dependence on God, they cannot operate as well as they could without further, divine enablement. On the other hand, since all gifts and talents ultimately trace their origin back to God's gracious hand, God is most honored and most pleased when we acknowledge this truth through prayer and trust in him as we use what he's given us.

Besides demonstrating his humility publicly, Daniel expressed it privately: he humbled himself by asking his friends for prayer. *A humble person seeks the help of others.* What is the first thing he does after he informs his friends of their dire predicament? "He urged them to plead for mercy from the God of heaven concerning this mystery, so that he and his friends might not be executed with the rest of the wise men of Babylon" (v. 18). Asking someone for help is humbling (that's why men never ask for directions!). Asking someone to pray for you can be humbling: it's an admission of vulnerability and personal need. Just after he became the new pontiff, one of the first things that people quickly noticed about Pope Francis was his humility: he asked the faithful to pray for him, rather than the other way around.

Sometimes we think that all as long as we are the ones praying for something, we don't need anybody else praying for us. When I was a pastor

Walking in Humility

in Ottawa I used to attend monthly prayer and fellowship gatherings for pastors in my denomination. After a time of worship and a devotional, we would go around the table and share prayer requests. I always found it odd that one particular pastor never had any prayer requests. He would always say something like, "No, I have no requests; it's all good." That always struck me as strange because, as a pastor, how could you not have prayer requests? How could you not ask for prayer for God's direction in your ministry, for anointing to preach, for a deeper love for the congregation, or for a dozen other things? It didn't surprise me, then, when I learned that that same pastor ended up resigning under duress from his church less than a year later.

True humility recognizes not only that we need God, but that because God has designed us to live in close fellowship with believers—the body of Christ—we also need each other. And perhaps the simplest expression of our need for other believers is asking them to pray for us. Even Jesus, who lived a life of complete and utter dependence on the Father, when he was struggling with his destiny on the cross, asked his closest disciples, Peter, James, and John, to pray with him in the Garden of Gethsemane (Matt 26:36-46 and parallels). A humble person seeks the help of others.

After God revealed the dream and its meaning to Daniel, Daniel was given an audience with King Nebuchadnezzar during which we observe another public display of his humble spirit. When the king asked Daniel if he is able to give the content of the dream and its interpretation, a not-so-humble person would have answered something like, "Actually, yes, I can; I have the gift of dream interpretation." But not Daniel. Daniel replied, "No wise man, enchanter, magician or diviner can explain to the king the mystery he has asked about, but there is a God in heaven who reveals mysteries. He has shown King Nebuchadnezzar what will happen in days to come" (vv. 27-28). Two things are apparent from Daniel's response. First, he was quick to give credit where credit was due: yes, he had been given the ability to interpret dreams and visions, but it is only by God's sovereign grace and design that he could do so. Second, being the humble servant that he was, Daniel evaded the spotlight by putting his boss there: "[God] has made known to King Nebuchadnezzar what will happen in days to come." Because God had revealed the meaning of the dream to Daniel, Daniel actually knew what would happen in history before Nebuchadnezzar did, so he could have shared the interpretation by saying something like, "O king, this is what God told *me* about your dream. God told *me* that . . ." But humble Daniel would have none of that. He told the king that the

We've Lost. What Now?

God in heaven—Daniel's God—had spoken to the king about the future, something he reiterates at the end of his report (v. 45b). *A humble person doesn't seek the limelight.*

Consider this: Daniel was highly regarded by the angels—three times the angel Gabriel referred to him as "highly esteemed" (9:23; 10:10, 19). Furthermore, the prophet Ezekiel singled him out for his righteousness and his wisdom (Ezek 14:14, 20; 28:3). Yet Daniel reflected a much lower estimation of himself before the king: "As for me, this mystery has been revealed to me, not because I have greater wisdom than anyone else alive, but so that Your Majesty may know the interpretation and that you may understand what went through your mind" (v. 30). Humble Daniel refused to hog the spotlight. He rather preferred his king enjoy it.

After reporting the content of the king's dream, when Daniel began to give its interpretation he once again demonstrated his humble spirit. We are explicitly told that "During the night the mystery was revealed to Daniel in a vision" (v. 19a), something Daniel affirmed (v. 30). Yet, when offering the all-important interpretation to Nebuchadnezzar, Daniel said, "This was the dream, and now we will interpret it to the king" (v. 36, also v. 23c). Why "we"? After all, the story makes it clear that Daniel stood alone before the king (vv. 24–26). Why then did Daniel say "we"? I think that unassuming Daniel was crediting his friends, Hananiah, Mishael, and Azariah, for they were the ones he turned to for prayer support and God answered their prayers.

Not too long ago a fad developed in the National Basketball Association. In years gone by, after a player scored a basket he would often point to the teammate who passed him the ball, in so doing deflecting the credit for the score to the other player—essentially saying, "Thanks for making me look good." Numerous players, however, began a trend whereby after scoring a basket, the player would look into the camera, grab his jersey and tug it—the NBA equivalent of "popping your collar." Thus the player, rather than deflect the credit for the basket to the one making the assist, proudly claimed all the glory for himself—"Look at me, I'm so great!" If Daniel played in the NBA he would obviously have been a "pointer" (deflecting the credit to his three friends who had been praying for him) and not a "popper" ("Look what I can do!").

In Daniel we see an extraordinarily gifted young man with an equally extraordinary spirit of humility. Not only did he stand out among the wise men of the kingdom for his immense giftedness, he stood out because of his great humility. While it is doubtless that it was because of Daniel's ability that the king would elevate him over the kingdom, we know that ultimately it was because of his humble spirit that God honored him with this promotion. "For all those who exalt themselves will be humbled, and those who humble themselves will be exalted."

Jesus declared that arrogant people (i.e., those who exalt themselves) will be *humbled*. He did not say that they will be *humble*. There's an enormous difference. Just because someone has been humbled doesn't mean that s/he is now humble. Haughty people periodically experience humiliating circumstances while continuing along steeped in their pride. For the past couple of decades God has been trying to get the attention of an extremely arrogant person I know quite well—by humbling him. His sterling business went under, causing him to accrue massive debt in an attempt to keep it afloat. When he eventually found another job, he resumed his rapid rise to corporate greatness. But years later he and the entire division he ran were suddenly dismissed—despite far exceeding his company's monetary expectations—because of corporate downsizing. Ten years later he has still not come even remotely close to finding another corporate position on par with his previous status. He has been humbled. God has humbled him! Yet those of us who know my friend well will tell you that he is still not a humble man. He is no more humble today than when he was proudly perched atop the corporate world. He has been humbled—like Jesus said— but he is not humble.

Through social, moral, and cultural exile God has humbled his church. But are we humble because of it? Because we have been pushed to the periphery, and because the church is taunted and hated in some quarters, it's easy for us to turn inward and become not simply hardened towards our society but actually arrogant. We all too easily speak or think ill of hair that's too long or pants that are too baggy, of people who watch a lot of movies or listen to certain types of music, and of people who work at blue-collar jobs or struggle to find employment. Truth be told, we look down on these people because they're not like us—and deep down we think they should be. So rather than acting compassionately towards them we arrogantly withhold mercy from them. And so our pride supplies fuel for the fire of our exile.

The Bible says explicitly that God opposes the proud (see Prov 3:34; Jas 4:6; 1 Pet 5:5). Whenever God humbles us, the crucial thing is this: How will we respond to him in the midst of our humiliating circumstances? Do we continue along in our arrogant way, keeping up appearances, business as usual? Or, do we humbly recognize our lowliness before God—that we're not as great as we think we really are? Do we acknowledge our deep-seated need for him in order to live the lives he desires us to live? The Scripture continues: "God opposes the proud . . . but shows favor to the humble." The difference, then, between being humbled and *being humble* is the difference between experiencing divine opposition and receiving God's grace. The author of Hebrews puts it like this: "Let us then approach the throne of grace with confidence, so that we may receive mercy and find grace to help us in our time of need" (Heb 4:16). God humbles us so that we might recognize our immense need for him and turn to him: not, in the first instance, to be rescued from our financial woes, or joblessness, or the like, but to receive his mercy and grace in order to become even more like Jesus during our time of need. The church has definitely been humbled through exile. But now we must *become humble* because of our exile.

Before we leave this chapter, there is an important subtext that pertains to King Nebuchadnezzar, and it is this: God speaks to unbelievers. While believers can expect God to speak to them with much greater frequency and clarity, it should not come as a big surprise that God sovereignly chooses to speak to unbelievers. Many generations earlier, God spoke to a pagan king in a dream about taking Sarah away from Abraham (Gen 20:1–7); he spoke to Hagar, Sarah's Egyptian maidservant, about the welfare of her son Ishmael (Gen 21:17–18); he spoke in a dream to an Egyptian cupbearer and baker about their respective futures (Gen 40:1–23). In Matthew's account of the Passion narrative we read that God spoke to Pilate's wife in a dream about Jesus' innocence (Matt 27:19). It would seem, then, that believers haven't cornered the market on hearing from God.

But why would God speak to unbelievers? Isaiah 26:10 sheds some light on this question: "Though grace is shown to the wicked, they do not learn righteousness; even in a land of uprightness they go on doing evil and regard not the majesty of the LORD." The inference from this verse is that God shows grace to the wicked so that they might learn of his righteousness and his majesty. Similarly, when preaching to the Athenian philosophers, Paul declared:

> From one man [God] made all the nations, that they should inhabit the whole earth; and he marked out their appointed times in history and the boundaries of their lands. God did this so that

they would seek him and perhaps reach out for him and find him,
though he is not far from any one of us. (Acts 17:26–27)

I believe that God blesses unbelievers in various ways so that they might come to recognize who he is so that they might seek him. Jesus said that our heavenly Father seeks after people who will worship him (John 4:23). We will observe this truth with the Babylonian king as the story of Daniel continues to unfold. Despite Nebuchadnezzar being the source of Israel's plight in the exile, God was pursuing him for a personal relationship. And to this end Daniel's life message would serve as a catalyst.

Likewise, I believe that God is actively pursuing some of our "captors"—those people in power who have helped toss the church to society's fringes. Just as Daniel's life served as a catalyst in God's pursuit of Nebuchadnezzar, our lives should also act as catalysts for God as he pursues the unbelievers around us for a personal relationship with himself.

Questions for Further Reflection

1. Is it hard for you to ask for prayer? When is it hardest? What makes it so difficult?

2. What are some ways that you can express your humility publicly? How about privately?

3. What does it look like when a local church is humble? What does an arrogant church look like?

4. What are some ways that a church congregation can practice or walk in humility towards outsiders?

5. In what ways does God communicate with unbelievers? Do you know any unbelievers to whom you think God may be speaking? How can you help them hear what God has to say to them?

3

Showing Commitment

Peter and the other apostles replied: "We must obey God rather than human beings!"

—ACTS 5:29

Failure is not for the faint of heart. By the age of thirty-five he had been defeated twice when he ran for a seat in Congress. Although he won two years later, he lost his re-election bid. At the age of forty-two, he was rejected for a land officer role. At forty-five, he ran for the Senate and lost. At forty-seven, he was defeated for the nomination for Vice President. At forty-nine, he ran for the Senate—again—and lost—again. At the age of fifty-one, he was elected President of the United States of America, eventually winning a second term in office, only to have that term cut short by an assassin's bullet. Despite his string of losses, Abraham Lincoln lives on as one of the all-time greats in US history.[1] His thoroughgoing commitment to serve his nation through public office enabled him to weather the storms of failure.

A lack of commitment can produce (among other things) fickleness. Here in our story we see the fickleness of the great King Nebuchadnezzar. At the end of chapter 2, the king made what could perhaps be construed as a profession of faith:

---

1. Staton, *Heaven-Bound Living*, 43–44.

We've Lost. What Now?

> Then King Nebuchadnezzar fell prostrate before Daniel and paid him honor and ordered that an offering and incense be presented to him. The king said to Daniel, "Surely your God is the God of gods and the Lord of kings and a revealer of mysteries, for you were able to reveal this mystery." (2:46–47)

You would think that after recognizing this grand truth—viz., that Daniel's God is far greater than the Babylonian gods—the king would be well on his way to embracing Daniel's God as his own. You would think that.

But, alas, kings—even great ones—are not impervious to being fickle:

> King Nebuchadnezzar made an image of gold, sixty cubits high and six cubits wide, and set it up on the plain of Dura in the province of Babylon. He then summoned the satraps, prefects, governors, advisers, treasurers, judges, magistrates and all the other provincial officials to come to the dedication of the image he had set up. So the satraps, prefects, governors, advisers, treasurers, judges, magistrates and all the other provincial officials assembled for the dedication of the image that King Nebuchadnezzar had set up, and they stood before it. (3:1–3)

For Daniel's original Jewish audience, the phrase "an image of gold" would probably have brought to mind the golden calf incident that took place in the wilderness under Aaron's tutelage (see Exodus 32). The author mentions three times in these verses that King Nebuchadnezzar is the one responsible for the construction of this image of gold.

And just like with the Israelites in the desert, idolatrous worship is involved:

> Then the herald loudly proclaimed, "Nations and peoples of every language, this is what you are commanded to do: As soon as you hear the sound of the horn, flute, zither, lyre, harp, pipe and all kinds of music, you must fall down and worship the image of gold that King Nebuchadnezzar has set up. Whoever does not fall down and worship will immediately be thrown into a blazing furnace." (3:4–6)

It would appear, then, that while Nebuchadnezzar had confessed with his mouth that Daniel's God was "the God of gods and the Lord of kings," his heart believed otherwise. How else could he have instituted such a vainglorious edict?

During the days of his earthly ministry, Jesus encountered fickle people. John writes, "many people saw the signs he was performing and

Showing Commitment

believed in his name. But Jesus would not entrust himself to them, for he knew all people" (John 2:23b–24). According to John, Jesus recognized the ease with which people can say one thing but in reality believe and live the polar opposite. Clearly, despite his profession of faith, Nebuchadnezzar had not come to believe in the God of Israel in a genuine way.

Soon after this latest imperial decree, some members of the king's court reveal to Nebuchadnezzar that his newly appointed provincial administrators, Shadrach, Meshach, and Abednego, have rejected his edict (vv. 8–12). Now, we could ask, what about Daniel? Where was he in all this? I will return to this question in chapter 5. Filled with rage, the king summons the threesome and orders them to give an account of their (good) behavior, threatening them with the furnace of fire if they still refuse to obey. Their response to the king is priceless:

> "King Nebuchadnezzar, we do not need to defend ourselves before you in this matter. If we are thrown into the blazing furnace, the God we serve is able to deliver us from it, and he will deliver us from Your Majesty's hand. But even if he does not, we want you to know, Your Majesty, that we will not serve your gods or worship the image of gold you have set up." (vv. 16–18).

Can't you just see the group's spokesperson sticking his finger in the king's chest?

I think it's pretty clear that these three young exiles possessed an *unwavering commitment to God*. Far from being irrational, this commitment was clearly a principled one. To begin with, *they trusted in God's power*: "the God we serve is able to deliver us." The Bible's story of how God works redemption on behalf of his people is replete with illustrations of his amazing power: the creation of the universe, the exodus from Egypt, the crossing of the Jordan River—just to name three. The psalmist aptly summarized it this way: "You are the God who performs miracles; you display your power among the peoples" (Ps 77:14). I cannot count how many times I've heard Christians testify to the powerful working of God in their circumstances. Of my three degrees, my final one (my PhD) was by far the most expensive venture because by that time I was financially supporting an entire family. And yet, God provided so amazingly for us during that time that we emerged from it completely debt free, in contrast to my other two degrees! Shadrach, Meshach, and Abednego knew of God's power, and consequently they possessed an unwavering commitment to him.

They trusted in God's goodness: "he will rescue us from your hand, O king." God, in his very essence, is good. When Moses asked God to show him his glory, the Lord responded, "I will cause all of my goodness to pass in front of you" (Exod 33:19a). Numerous psalmists sing songs testifying to God's goodness:

> Taste and see that the Lord is good; blessed is the one who takes refuge in him. (Ps 34:8)

> You, Lord, are forgiving and good, abounding in love to all who call to you. (Ps 86:5)

> You are good, and what you do is good. (Ps 119:68a)

> Praise the Lord, for the Lord is good; sing praise to his name, for that is pleasant. (Ps 135:3)

> Give thanks to the Lord, for he is good. His love endures forever. (Ps 136:1)

Because God is good, he delights in using his power to bring blessing into the lives of his people. Doubtless Shadrach, Meshach, and Abednego had experienced this truth, and therefore they could remain steadfast in their commitment to God.

They trusted in God's sovereignty: "But even if he does not." God is all-powerful. God is perfect in goodness. Yet sometimes bad things happen—something to which the Scriptures themselves attest. But rather than doubting God's power, or doubting God's goodness, the biblical authors respond to this dilemma (viz., why bad things happen to good people) by resolutely trusting in God's sovereignty and in his infinite wisdom. I will return to this theme in greater detail in chapter 7. For now, I simply point out that the trio's "even if he does not" response is reminiscent of Jesus' at his arrest. When the mob advanced to capture Jesus, and Peter tried to defend him by slicing off the high priest's slave's ear, Jesus responded, "Put your sword back in its place. . . . Do you think I cannot call on my Father, and he will at once put at my disposal more than twelve legions of angels? But how then would the Scriptures be fulfilled that say it must happen in this way?" (Matt 26:52–54). Jesus knew that God had the power to save him from what was about to happen. But rather than demand rescue from God, he chose to trust in God's sovereign plan for his life—viz., the crucifixion.

Invariably this kind of trust manifests in the threesome's unwavering commitment: "we will not serve your gods or worship the image of gold

Showing Commitment

you have set up" (v. 18b). I believe that it was this commitment that had prompted Daniel and his three friends' resolution not to defile themselves with the royal food and wine earlier in the story (1:8).

Superficiality breeds fickleness, but *an unwavering commitment to God produces consistency*—in behaviour and in character. And consistency is measured in years, not days. After he had been imprisoned, John the Baptist began to doubt if Jesus was the Messiah. John the Baptist—the man who, when baptizing Jesus, immediately recognized the Lord's superiority; the one who, when he saw Jesus approaching, declared, "Behold the lamb of God who takes away the sin of the world"—this same John began to have doubts about Jesus. So he sent some of his disciples to question Jesus. After reaffirming his messianic identity to John, Jesus anticipated what the crowds were now thinking about his cousin—viz., that this great prophet of judgment was, in reality, fickle. But Jesus would have none of this:

> Jesus began to speak to the crowd about John: "What did you go out into the wilderness to see? A reed swayed by the wind? If not, what did you go out to see? . . . A prophet? Yes, I tell you, and more than a prophet. . . . Truly I tell you, among those born of women there has not risen anyone greater than John the Baptist." (Matt 11:7b–11a)

John was not fickle. Although John had his doubts in that particular instance, over the course of his life he had been consistent in his witness. He had an unwavering commitment to God that produced in him a consistent character, and would eventually cost him his life.

I'm sure Nebuchadnezzar thought that Shadrach, Meshach, and Abednego's commitment to their God would cost them their lives. But it did not. God sovereignly intervened and rescued them from the fire (vv. 19–27). Consequently, Nebuchadnezzar made another confession of sorts:

> Praise be to the God of Shadrach, Meshach and Abednego . . . Therefore I decree that the people of any nation or language who say anything against the God of Shadrach, Meshach and Abednego be cut into pieces and their houses be turned into piles of rubble, for no other god can save in this way. (vv. 28a, 29)

I believe there were two factors that prompted the king's profession here. First and most obviously, was God's miraculous intervention: Nebuchadnezzar recognized that God had "sent his angel and rescued his servants" (v. 28). According to John's Gospel, Jesus affirmed that miracles could act as catalysts for faith: "Believe me when I say that I am in the Father and the Father is in me; or at least believe on the evidence of the works themselves" (John 14:11). While miracles do not necessarily call forth faith (see, for example, Matt 11:20–24, where Jesus condemns the unbelieving, unrepentant cities where he had performed most of his miracles), sometimes they do elicit some measure of faith, as they appear to do here in Daniel's story.

The second and not so obvious factor that prompted Nebuchadnezzar's confession was Shadrach, Meshach, and Abednego's unwavering commitment to God. The king declared, "They trusted in him and defied the king's command and were willing to give up their lives rather than serve or worship any god except their own God" (v. 28b). While the king had been fickle, the three exiles were anything but. Nebuchadnezzar had heard the words that came forth from their commitment; the king's ears probably still rang from their powerful words of rebuke:

> "King Nebuchadnezzar, we do not need to defend ourselves before you in this matter. If we are thrown into the blazing furnace, the God we serve is able to deliver us from it, and he will deliver us from Your Majesty's hand. But even if he does not, we want you to know, Your Majesty, that we will not serve your gods or worship the image of gold you have set up." (vv. 16–18).

And his chest probably still hurt from having an index finger stuck in it!

But he also *saw* their commitment. Far from being empty words, the trio's actions—or more precisely, their willingness to be thrown into the fire—fully backed up their words. That impressed Nebuchadnezzar. Because of the divine intervention, he issued a decree in support of the God of the Jews. But it was, I think, because of the character of their commitment to God that he rewarded them: "Then the king promoted Shadrach, Meshach, and Abednego in the province of Babylon" (v. 30).

Our world is filled with people who appear to be upstanding, positive contributors to society, but in reality they lack any kind of moral compass. The financial scandals of the previous decade have brought this hidden reality to light—Enron, Adelphia Communications, Bre-X, Parmalat, Bear Stearns, Lehman Brothers, Bernie Madoff, and the list goes on. Looking back on those scandals, Linda Davies, former Wall Street investment banker turned financial thriller novelist, told an audience at an Economic and Monetary Union Conference in Amsterdam, "Bankers who hire money hungry geniuses should not always express surprise and amazement when

Showing Commitment

some of them turn around with brilliant, creative, and illegal means of making money."[2]

On May 25, 2006, a jury convicted former Enron CEOs Kenneth Lay and Jeffrey Skilling of multiple counts of conspiracy and fraud in one of the biggest business scandals in US history. While these extremely gifted men transformed a staid pipeline company into the seventh-largest corporation (at its peak), it seemed clear to the jury that their moral compasses had broken somewhere along the road to success. Each man took the witness stand to deploy their legendary salesmanship on their own behalf. One juror testified after the verdict, "I wanted very, very badly to believe what they were saying, but there were places in their testimony where I felt their character was questioned." I believe that character stems from a clear moral commitment to truth.

Doubtless the leading culprits in these scandals secretly flaunted their immoral and corrupt activities. And while a lot of us condemn their acts, sadly, few would condone the attitude that led to their wrongdoing. The biggest offence for many of us was merely the extent to which these people had lied and cheated in order to secure personal gain—not the self-entitlement attitude that invariably drove these executives to commit their crimes. In other words, lying and cheating "a little" for personal gain is okay, but doing it to the extent these people did is not.

While the world often mocks people who possess strong morals, I firmly believe that it, ironically, respects and values people with a strong moral commitment—one that trumps the desire for personal gain and glory. The *Hamilton Spectator* published an article entitled, "Reinvesting in God" (March 11, 2009) by Joan Walters. Walters interviewed Jonathan Wellum, the CEO of the multibillion-dollar company AIC Ltd., in the wake of the Wall Street meltdown. Wellum declared:

> [While] selfishness, materialism and a need for instant gratification drove the markets and played out in the economy for years.... Now, we need men and women with purpose, who think long-term, who draw lines, who stand on fixed principles, unwavering, disciplined, treating each other with the highest respect.[3]

My late father was a mechanic (a mechanic's mechanic, you could say). I remember while driving with him on one occasion he told me a story of

---

2. Davies, "Psychology of Risk, Speculation and Fraud."
3. Waters, "Reinvesting in God."

what had happened to him recently. He had sold a car to man who returned a few days later complaining that the car had a faulty clutch. Dad knew that there was nothing wrong with the clutch when he sold him the car, but he fixed it anyway, free of charge. A few days later the man returned again with the same complaint. This sounded suspicious, so my dad had the man drive his own car, while he observed in the passenger seat. Dad saw that the man didn't actually know how to drive a manual transmission correctly: he rode the clutch and that's why he was experiencing his problems. So my dad did two things: he fixed the clutch again—at no charge—and he taught the man how to drive a standard properly. A lesser man would have charged both times—after all, there's money to be had. And a lesser man would not have wasted his time teaching this chap how to drive—after all, time is money! The only people who don't appreciate a commitment to doing the right thing are the people whose vain pursuit of gain and glory gets in the way of doing the right thing.

Society might not want (what it perceives to be) the religiosity that often accompanies a strong moral commitment to truth, but it nevertheless desires the essence that our faith offers: a deep moral commitment through which other people can tangibly benefit. Christians in living exile have ample opportunity to model the value of commitment to their "captors." In the workplace: in the high tech age in which we live, time theft has become a problem for many employers that is nearly as widespread as the common cold. Time theft involves pursuing our own personal interests at the expense our employer's needs. The Christian employee knows that to honor your contract to your employer is, ultimately, to honor God (Col 3:22–24).

In school: some time ago a survey in *US News & World Report* recorded that 75 percent of college students admitted to cheating, and 85 percent of college students said cheating was necessary to get ahead. A student committed to personal gain and glory, then, will cheat—they have to if they want to get ahead (so they think). The student with a strong moral compass, however, will not cheat. Even if "everybody's doing it," that still doesn't make it right; and in fact, because it's not the right thing to do, the Christian student will, therefore, avoid cheating.

In the family: the reason why some marriages disintegrate is because one partner values his/her career and the glory that can come from it, over his/her spouse; s/he has chosen to commit to a thing rather than to a person. The reason why some kids go AWOL is because their fathers are far more committed to achieving worldly success than to being a good dad;

they are more committed to experiencing personal comfort than to enduring the hard, often thankless labor of parenting.

Commitment is costly. It often costs us time and effort, money and marks, status and comfort, tears and pain. Commitment to God ultimately cost Jesus his life. In fact, it is still costing Christians their lives in some parts of the world today. Some people avoid commitment like the plague (like Ryan from *The Office*), but everyone wants to enjoy the fruit that comes from commitment. By showing itself as a community of commitment, comprised of a people committed to God, to his values, and to each other, the exilic church can offer the world a witness to a way of life that might seem foreign to them, but they can nevertheless taste and enjoy the fruit born of that commitment, and thus be drawn (even if imperceptibly) closer to the Truth.

Questions for Further Reflection

1. What are some things that you're committed to? How does your commitment to these things show up in your life, i.e., what's the evidence of your commitment to these things?

2. Who are some people you're committed to? How do you express your commitment to them? Can these people easily recognize your commitment to them?

3. Are you committed to God? How do you express your commitment to him? Under what kind of circumstances do you find it difficult to express your commitment to God? Why do you think that is? Are there ways that you can strengthen your commitment to God?

4. What are some ways that you can model to outsiders a commitment to the truth?

5. What does commitment look like in the life of a local church? What does a lack of commitment look like? What does it mean for a church to express its commitment against social or political pressures? Are there places or issues where the church can do this?

4

Genuinely Caring

For God does speak—now one way, now another—though no one perceives it.

—JOB 33:14

In *The Workbook on Living as a Christian*, Maxie Dunnam describes a scene at the funeral of former US Vice President Hubert Humphrey. Hundreds of people from across the world attended his funeral. All were welcome but one: former President Richard Nixon, who had not long previously dragged himself and his country through the humiliation and shame of Watergate. As eyes turned away and conversations ran dry around him, Nixon could feel the ostracism being ladled out to him. Then Jimmy Carter, the President at the time, walked into the room. Carter was from a different political party to Nixon and known for his honesty and integrity. President Carter, as he moved to his seat, noticed Richard Nixon standing all alone. Carter immediately changed course, walked over to Nixon, held out his hand, and smiling genuinely and broadly embraced Nixon and said, "Welcome home, Mr. President! Welcome home!" The incident was reported in *Newsweek* magazine: "If there was a turning point in Nixon's long ordeal in the wilderness, it was that moment and that gesture of love and compassion."[1]

---

1. Dunnam, *Workbook*, 112–13.

We've Lost. What Now?

Previously I mentioned that God can and does at times speak to unbelievers. The reason he does is so that they might come to recognize who he is, turn to him through repentance, and enter into a personal relationship with him. God had been relationally pursuing King Nebuchadnezzar. He began to pursue the king (at least, as far as we know) by speaking to him in an enigmatic dream in which God revealed the future of the Babylonian Empire to Nebuchadnezzar (Dan 2:1–45). We don't know for sure what kind of beliefs about the God of the Jews Nebuchadnezzar had prior to this divine revelation, but after Daniel interpreted it for him, he confessed to Daniel, "Surely your God is the God of gods and the Lord of kings" (2:47). The third chapter of Daniel, however, exposed the superficiality of this confession: although Nebuchadnezzar had made a kind of profession of faith, he did not yet fully embrace Daniel's faith. Nor did he even have a grasp of the implications of his confession of God's sovereignty. Yet God continued to pursue the king.

After throwing Shadrach, Meshach, and Abednego into the fiery furnace, Nebuchadnezzar saw a mysterious figure that he insisted looked like "a son of the gods," walking around with the three exiles in the furnace, protecting them from harm. From receiving a prophetic dream to experiencing an angelophany (i.e., the manifestation of an angel in the physical realm), there seems to be an escalation in the intensity of God's communication with Nebuchadnezzar. As a result of this heightened interaction, the king issued a decree that forbade people from speaking against the God of the Jews (3:29). This was another positive confession of sorts, but Nebuchadnezzar was not quite there—he still stood outside of the boundaries of a genuine faith-relationship with God. But as we shall see, God was about to ramp up his communiqué with the king.

Chapter 4 takes the form of a letter from Nebuchadnezzar to his kingdom:

> It is my pleasure to tell you about the miraculous signs and wonders that the Most High God has performed for me. How great are his signs, how mighty his wonders! His kingdom is an eternal kingdom; his dominion endures from generation to generation. (vv. 2–3)

Up to this point in the narrative, Nebuchadnezzar had only issued statements about God or what perhaps could be considered indirect praise. For example, when he exclaimed to Daniel, "Surely your God is the God of gods and the Lord of kings and a revealer of mysteries" (2:47), he did not address God directly but only spoke about God. Similarly, after the furnace incident the king declared, "Praise be to the God of Shadrach, Meshach and Abednego, who has sent his angel and rescued his servants" (3:28a). Again, he spoke about God but not to God. But here in the opening of chapter 4, Nebuchadnezzar addressed God more directly and not simply as the God of someone else: "It is my pleasure to tell you about [what] the Most High God has performed for me." The bulk of chapter 4 describes how the king had come to this place of a newfound perspective about Daniel's God.

Nebuchadnezzar had another disturbing dream that frightened him. As before, he summoned the wise men to interpret it. But this time he went easier on them: they only had to interpret the dream without having first to recount its content; additionally, he did not threaten to execute them if they failed to interpret his dream correctly. Perhaps he was just getting soft in his old age. Unfortunately, the wise men still could not do it. Enter Daniel.

From past experience Nebuchadnezzar knew that if anybody could interpret his dream it would be Daniel. So when Daniel approached him, Nebuchadnezzar didn't ask him if he was able to interpret it—like he did the first time. He simply said, "Here is my dream; interpret it for me" (v. 9b). Further, the basis for the king's confidence in Daniel rested not in his interpretive abilities, per se, but in the source of his ability: "none of the wise men in my kingdom can interpret it for me. But you can, because the spirit of the holy gods is in you" (v. 18).

After the king revealed the substance of his dream, the NIV says that Daniel's thoughts "terrified him" (v. 19a). Some Bible translations soften the rendering to "troubled" (KJV/NKJV), "worried" (CEV), or "alarmed" (ESV). This section of the book of Daniel (2:4—7:25), unlike most of the Old Testament, was originally written in Aramaic, a close sister language to biblical Hebrew. The Aramaic word that the NIV translates "terrified" occurs only here; literally it means "be appalled." The Hebrew equivalent of this word does appear throughout the Old Testament, often connoting "fear." Thus, for example, the equivalent Hebrew word is used to describe the reaction of Joseph's brothers after he revealed his identity to them: when Joseph's brothers, who had maliciously jumped him and sold him into slavery, found out that their little brother had become the second most powerful political leader in the world and was now in a perfect position to exact his vengeance upon them, they were "not able to answer [Joseph] because they were *terrified* at his presence" (Gen 45:3b). Similarly, the woman of Endor observed that King Saul was *"greatly shaken"* by the ominous news, delivered by the ghost of Samuel (we won't go there), of his imminent demise at the hands of the Philistines (1 Sam 28:21). In each instance, fear is associated with the word. Well, when Daniel heard the king's dream, he immediately knew what it meant—that it spelled bad news for the king—which is why "his thoughts terrified him" (v. 19b). So he said to Nebuchadnezzar, "My lord, if only the dream applied to your enemies"—or, as the BBE translates it, "your haters"—"and its meaning to your adversaries!" (v. 19c).

The substance of the dream can be summarized as follows: God had caused Nebuchadnezzar's kingdom and greatness to grow beyond imagination. Researchers have shown that Nebuchadnezzar was the greatest monarch that Babylon (perhaps even the Ancient Near East generally) ever produced. He appears to have built or restored almost every city and temple in the entire country. His vast kingdom was equally known for its immense splendor. Ninety percent of Babylon was composed of bricks stamped with his name. One ancient historian claimed that the outer walls of his city were three 320 high and 80 feet thick (wide enough to allow a four-horse chariot to turn on them, according to the historian). Inside these massive walls were fortresses and temples containing huge statues of solid gold. One of the city's most spectacular sites was the Hanging Gardens of Babylon, considered one of the Seven Wonders of the Ancient World. These vaulted stone terraces were, according to some ancient reports, 400 feet wide by 400 feet long and more than 80 feet high. Clearly, Nebuchadnezzar had experienced greatness beyond imagination. But because Nebuchadnezzar believed that his immense glory and status came directly as the result of his own power, his own wisdom, and his own ingenuity, God was going to humble him by removing his sanity and driving him out of his kingdom to live in the wild with the animals, until he acknowledged that God alone is the true, sovereign power.

And this is exactly what happens in the final part of the chapter. One year after the dream, as Nebuchadnezzar was surveying his kingdom from the roof of his complex, he overflowed with self-admiration and exclaimed, "Is not this the great Babylon I have built as the royal residence, by my mighty power and for the glory of my majesty"? (v. 30). No sooner did these words roll off his tongue than God struck the king with insanity and drove him away from his kingdom.

The observation I would like to make at this point of the story is this: God had once again intensified his relational pursuit of Nebuchadnezzar. God first spoke to him in a dream concerning the future (ch. 2). Later God

Genuinely Caring

spoke to him through an angelophany: when Shadrach, Meshach, and Abednego were thrown into the furnace, Nebuchadnezzar saw an angelic figure in the fire protecting the trio from harm (ch. 3). So there is a heightened move in divine communication: from the realm of the subconscious (dreams) to the conscious, physical realm (the manifestation of an angel). Here in our text, there is a further intensification: from that which is less personal and external (i.e., what the king saw with his eyes, viz., an angel) to that which is more personal and internal (i.e., what he experiences in his own body and mind, viz., insanity). Why would God do this? Is God simply some power-drunk ogre who enjoys toying with people? Hardly. God was sovereignly and lovingly pursuing King Nebuchadnezzar for a personal relationship with himself. The arrogant king had rejected God's initial overtures but God is a persistent suitor: he merely stepped up his advances.

In the end, God finally got his man:

> At the end of that time, I, Nebuchadnezzar, raised my eyes toward heaven, and my sanity was restored. Then I praised the Most High; I honored and glorified him who lives forever. His dominion is an eternal dominion; his kingdom endures from generation to generation. . . . Now I, Nebuchadnezzar, praise and exalt and glorify the King of heaven, because everything he does is right and all his ways are just. And those who walk in pride he is able to humble. (vv. 34, 37)

These words sound like the song of a new convert! It took some doing: God had to turn up the heat (so to speak) to get his message across to the king. But Nebuchadnezzar had finally come around; he entered into a genuine, personal, faith-relationship with the God of Israel. Remember, this is the same Nebuchadnezzar who had been responsible for decimating the people of God, the sacred city of Jerusalem, and the holy temple, sending God's people away from the Promised Land into the ignominy of Babylonian exile. This is the same king who set up a huge image of gold and coerced all the people of his kingdom to worship it or face death.

This subplot of Daniel brings to mind a story from the other end of the Bible, the book of Acts. There Luke gives an account of a Pharisee named Saul of Tarsus, who zealously devoted his life to practising the Jewish religion to the point of feverishly striving to destroy the church of Jesus Christ (Acts 9). If ever there was a candidate for "Least likely to become a Christian," it was Saul of Tarsus. Yet Luke describes how the risen Lord met

Saul while he was on the Damascus Road seeking to arrest more of Jesus' followers (just another day in the life for Saul). Jesus met him, not to pour out well-deserved divine judgment upon him for all the terrible acts he had committed against Christians, but to welcome him into the Body of Christ. If God could lovingly pursue the self-proclaimed "chief of sinners," surely he could pursue a sot like Nebuchadnezzar. Clearly, no person stands outside the boundary lines of God's love. If God pursued a relationship with someone like Nebuchadnezzar, could it be that he is pursuing members of our society today who have and continue to contribute heavily to the marginalization of the church? Could God be pursuing members of the Prime Minister's Office? Members of the Opposition? Members of the White House? Senators? Heads of the media? Union leaders? Does anyone really stand outside of the boundary lines of God's love?

What strikes me about Daniel here is not so much his extraordinary giftedness, but his authentic concern for the king. He understood what the dream meant, was terrified by it, and reticent to give its interpretation. The king practically had to pry it out of him (v. 19c). And when Daniel finally shared its meaning with Nebuchadnezzar, he exclaimed, "My lord, if only the dream applied to your enemies and its meaning to your adversaries!" (v. 19c). Why did Daniel feel this way? Was he afraid that the interpretation would offend and enrage the king? While that is possible, I don't think that was what was going on. If that was so, then I don't think Daniel would have pleaded with the king to repent of his sins (v. 27).

I think the reason for Daniel's hesitancy with Nebuchadnezzar is that he genuinely cared for him. Again, Nebuchadnezzar was the reason Daniel and his people were living in exile outside of the Promised Land. He was the reason God's holy city and holy temple had been destroyed. He was the reason Daniel's best friends were nearly executed, if not for divine intervention. How easy it would have been for Daniel to give to the king the dream's interpretation with an air of smugness, knowing that Nebuchadnezzar's demise could spell, among other things, a return to the Promised Land. But not so with Daniel. He was genuinely concerned for his king's welfare. That is precisely why he wished that the dream had been for Nebuchadnezzar's "haters" and why he went on to offer the king his counsel in light of the dream: "Therefore, Your Majesty, be pleased to accept my advice: Renounce your sins by doing what is right, and your wickedness by being kind to the oppressed. It may be that then your prosperity will continue" (v. 27). Daniel's warning of repentance echoes the standard message of Israel's prophets to pagan kings, except for the last phrase: "It may be that then your prosperity will continue."

When preaching to foreign kings, God's prophets rarely if ever paid any mind to the personal well-being of their royal opponents. For example, in Isaiah's lengthy prophecy against the king of Tyre he expressed no concern for that king's welfare (Isa 14:3–23). The same can be said of Ezekiel in his prophecy against Pharaoh (Ezek 29:1–16). The last part of Daniel's counsel to Nebuchadnezzar, viz., wishing for his continued prosperity, only makes sense if Daniel genuinely cared for his king.

Like Daniel, *we must genuinely care for the unbelievers God places in our life*. It becomes all too easy for an exiled community—a community that has been thrust from society's center to its fringes, becoming an object of scorn and contempt—to circle the wagons and stop caring about the world, be concerned only about itself, and adopt a club mentality. And, truth be told, it feels good to be a part of an exclusive club, doesn't it? I can remember forming a neighbourhood spy club as a child. It was small, of course, but, boy, did we have lots of fun! We had our own secret greeting and language of communication. Our common interests brought us together and bound us together. We were never interested in getting any bigger, so we never advertised or marketed our club. Very occasionally we let someone in (like maybe once) but that was always the exception and never the rule. We were quite happy and content to keep things the way they were.

When my wife and I moved to Hamilton to begin my doctoral studies in 2002, we looked for a new church home. Sadly, we discovered that this club mentality exists in the typical evangelical church. We visited many churches—different sizes, denominations, traditions, locales—but always (with rare exception) the same experience: a cold, unfriendly reception. These churches reserved their greetings for their own members; their shared experiences and inside jokes were kept to their own circles. The sign outside might have read, "Visitors welcome," but these churches sent a clear and direct message based on their body language: "New people are not welcome!" Now, being Christians, for my wife and I to get a frosty reception at a church was, ultimately, no big deal. We just crossed that church off our list and moved on to the next. But what about the non-Christian who, after many years, bravely decides to give church a try? The chances of that person taking their chilly rejection in stride and simply trying out another church are next to zero. When a community becomes socially and culturally marginalized, the natural inclination can be to retreat from the world, circle the wagons, and live in holy huddles. Daniel didn't do that.

Having lost the high ground and having become derisively trampled underneath society's feet, it becomes easy for the church to begin to despair. After all, we've lost, so what's the point? And it is this grave sense of doom and gloom that can reinforce a club mentality. It can also cause people to pine away for the "good old days," or to fixate on the future—the Second Coming and heaven—to such an extent that we lose our saltiness and allow our light to grow dim. But being salt, as Jesus admonished (Matt 5:13), actually presupposes close contact with corruptive forces—otherwise there would be no need for salt. Similarly, light expressly exists for the darkness (Matt 5:14–16). We can never allow our social and cultural marginalization to stop us, for example, from heeding Paul's counsel to Timothy to pray diligently for our political leaders (1 Tim 2:1–4)—especially when those same leaders continue to deconstruct traditional, biblical values, sometimes mocking the church in the process.

Let Daniel be our example. King Nebuchadnezzar was directly responsible for the devastation of the holy city of Jerusalem, the destruction of God's sacred temple, the ruthless slaughter of thousands of Israelites, and the "kidnapping" and transporting of many thousands more to Babylonia. If ever someone was justified to retreat to a secret inner circle, to be overcome with despair, and to pine away for the good old days, it was Daniel. But he did not allow the exile to choke out his care, his concern, or his compassion for Nebuchadnezzar. While the text does not mention it, I would find it hard to believe, given what we know of Daniel, that he didn't pray sincerely and regularly for his king. Perhaps one of the most caring things exilic believers can do for their captors—be they politicians, union leaders, or members of the media—is to heed the words of Jesus: "But I tell you, love your enemies and pray for those who persecute you" (Matt 5:44). Genuine care and concern for our society begins simply with diligent, loving, intercessory prayer on their behalf.

Questions for Further Reflection

1. Have you ever felt like God was not interested in saving certain individuals? Like who? In light of the experiences of people like

Genuinely Caring

Nebuchadnezzar and Saul of Tarsus, can you really believe that this is the case?

2. In what ways do you think God pursues these sorts of people? Is there something you can do to serve as a catalyst for God in his pursuit of these people?

3. Do you care for your "opponents," i.e., people with whom you disagree politically, socially, culturally, or ideologically? How do you or can you express your care for them?

4. How can the church show genuine care to a culture that generally rejects it?

5. What does it mean for the church to care for a post-Christendom society? Does post-Christendom care differ from Christendom care? In what ways?

5

Engaging with Excellence

Whatever you do, work at it with all your heart, as working for the Lord, not for human masters.

—COL 3:23

Former ESPN and *Monday Night Football* commentator Joe Theismann enjoyed a distinguished twelve-year career as an NFL quarterback for the Washington Redskins, winning the league MVP award and leading his team to two Super Bowl appearances, winning the first one in 1983, but losing the following year. Before a leg injury forced him out of football, he had become Washington's all-time leading passer. Not long after his retirement, in an interview with *The Washington Post Magazine*, Theismann shared a bitter lesson he had learned at the tail end of his career:

> I got stagnant. I thought the team revolved around me. I should have known it was time to go when I didn't care whether my pass hit Art Monk in the 8 or the 1 on his uniform. When we went back to the Super Bowl, my approach had changed. I was griping about the weather, my shoes, practice times, everything. Today I wear my two rings: the winner's ring from Super Bowl XVII and the loser's ring from Super Bowl XVIII. The difference in those two rings lies in applying oneself and not accepting anything but the best.[1]

1. Quoted from *Reader's Digest*, January 1992.

We've Lost. What Now?

The fifth chapter of Daniel seems somewhat out of place in the chronology of the narrative. The story's chronology would be better served if chapter 4 was followed by chapter 7 (which is set in the first year of King Belshazzar), then chapter 8 (which is set in the third year of Belshazzar), and then chapter 5 (which has no specific setting but ends with the overthrow of Belshazzar). However, the juxtaposition of chapters 4 and 5 has little to do with chronology and more to do with a character contrast. The previous chapter ended with the conversion of King Nebuchadnezzar after an extended period of humbling by God. The account of Nebuchadnezzar's positive response to God's pursuit of him is now contrasted with his successor's negative response to God's gracious act of communication.

The chapter opens with a grand banquet thrown by King Belshazzar; nothing unusual about that—that's what kings do. But it's what the king did at the banquet that would have caused the hairs on Daniel's original audience to stand on end:

> While Belshazzar was drinking his wine, he gave orders to bring in the gold and silver goblets that Nebuchadnezzar his father had taken from the temple in Jerusalem, so that the king and his nobles, his wives and his concubines might drink from them. So they brought in the gold goblets that had been taken from the temple of God in Jerusalem, and the king and his nobles, his wives and his concubines drank from them. As they drank the wine, they praised the gods of gold and silver, of bronze, iron, wood and stone. (vv. 2–4)

Back in the hey-day of Israel's monarchy, King David had dedicated his own personal treasures of gold and silver to the temple (1 Chr 29:3). King Solomon's wealth was so great that all of his goblets were gold because silver was actually considered of little value during his day (1 Kgs 10:21). But now, some pagan ruler has plundered God's temple in Jerusalem and taken these sacred vessels in order to toast his false gods. Upon hearing this, a pious Jew would have been seized with indignation. Little wonder, then, that the God of the Jews did not remain silent for long:

> Suddenly the fingers of a human hand appeared and wrote on the plaster of the wall, near the lampstand in the royal palace. The king watched the hand as it wrote. His face turned pale and he was so frightened that his legs became weak and his knees were knocking. (vv. 5–6)

Engaging with Excellence

In a panic, King Belshazzar summoned his wise men and offered them a great reward if they could interpret the writing on the wall (hmm, sound familiar?). Unfortunately for the king, none of his wise men could interpret the writing, and at this, "King Belshazzar became even more terrified and his face grew more pale" (v. 9). Fortunately for Belshazzar, behind every good man there's a good woman (although I guess in his case, behind some bad men there can be a good woman): the queen alerted her husband to someone she had heard about:

> There is a man in your kingdom who has the spirit of the holy gods in him. In the time of your father he was found to have insight and intelligence and wisdom like that of the gods. Your father, King Nebuchadnezzar, appointed him chief of the magicians, enchanters, astrologers and diviners. He did this because Daniel, whom the king called Belteshazzar, was found to have a keen mind and knowledge and understanding, and also the ability to interpret dreams, explain riddles and solve difficult problems. Call for Daniel, and he will tell you what the writing means. (vv. 11–12).

Over the course of time that he had worked in the royal court, Daniel had gained quite a reputation—one that would follow him even into the reign of the Persians (Dan 6:3). He was excellent at what he did. And *excellence serves as a positive witness to society*. Among King Nebuchadnezzar's counsellors, Daniel had so successfully served with distinction that even the wife of Nebuchadnezzar's successor had heard of him. And because of the queen's word, King Belshazzar had now heard of Daniel's sterling reputation, for he summoned Daniel and said, "I have heard that the spirit of the gods is in you and that you have insight, intelligence and outstanding wisdom. . . . Now I have heard that you are able to give interpretations and to solve difficult problems" (vv. 14, 16a). Clearly, Daniel's excellent reputation as a "problem solver" preceded him.

Excellence is well received by our Western culture, but the lack thereof, i.e., mediocrity, is (understandably) not. Back in the 1970s, Bill Hybels conducted a survey asking people what kept them away from church, the results of which shaped how he would go on to do ministry at what would become the famous mega-church, Willow Creek Community Church. According to the survey, one of the reasons people did not go to church was because the sermons were boring and irrelevant. While the gospel is by definition an "offence" (see Gal 5:11b), and while the Bible was not designed to tickle our ears or our funny bones, there is no excuse for poor and boring sermon delivery. Our pulpits are filled with too many preachers who lack the spiritual gift of preaching. I'm not saying you have to stand on your head (although for some preachers I've heard, that couldn't hurt), but what I am saying is that a solid delivery goes a long way.

I had a professor at seminary with whose theological positions—which he tended to teach rather aggressively—I strongly disagreed. A number of times I would come away from the end of his lectures feeling somewhat disturbed and quite frustrated. But you know what? I actually looked forward to attending his lectures, even more so than some professors' who shared my theological convictions. Why? All of my professors were veritable bottomless pits of theology, Greek, and Hebrew. But what set this professor apart from some of the others was his outstanding rhetorical ability. A great delivery goes a long way.

While excellence can serve as a beneficial witness to society, the motive for excellence is just as important because it reveals what's in the heart. What drove Daniel to want to be exceptional? We know from the text that it wasn't money or power: "Then Daniel answered the king, 'You may keep your gifts for yourself and give your rewards to someone else. Nevertheless, I will read the writing for the king and tell him what it means'" (v. 17). Daniel's drive to be extraordinary was not motivated by the promise of wealth, power, or prestige. How different Daniel is from the spirit of our age. Nowadays, people just want to get paid. I remember reading about one NBA all-star who, although making at the time fourteen million dollars per year, lamented, "Why should I help this team win a championship unless they're willing to pay me more money?" I guess fourteen million reasons aren't enough for some people.

Conventional wisdom believes that in order to attract the best and brightest employees you have to be willing to pay them exorbitantly. Thus, for example, in the world of politics, high-ranking government officials periodically claim that to attract the best people to politics they must be offered a compensation package comparable to what they would receive in the private sector. In a May 28, 2010, story, *The Hamilton Spectator* reported that when Air Canada increased its pool of available stocks to reward its executives, it did this "to attract, retain and motivate employees in key positions."[2] In other words, if you want people to excel you have to pay them. But never mind the debacle we observed in the corporate world last decade (and still today), viz., that money doesn't guarantee excellence. How

---

2. "Air Canada Rewards Execs."

many CEOs of large companies have been fired for poor job performance despite earning tens of millions of dollars? If money truly secures success that should never happen.

In 1993 the *Harvard Business Review* published an article by noted author, social science researcher, and lecturer Alfie Kohn that would prove prophetic for the corporate world in the subsequent decade. In his perceptive piece, "Why Incentive Plans Cannot Work," Kohn, based on his analysis of numerous studies, argued that incentives merely offer a short-term compliance rather than long-term change. The problem, he says, is that "[incentives] do not alter the attitudes that underlie our behaviors. They do not create an enduring *commitment* to any value or action. Rather, incentives merely—and temporarily—change what we do."[3] True excellence comes from within not from without. The people we acclaim to be the best fathers and mothers did not become the best because of the promise of money or fame. In fact, if nothing else, so-called reality TV shows us that money and fame can actually come to dysfunctional fathers and mothers. And while there may be an unspoken "rewards system" in some marriages, the people we generally consider to be the best husbands or the best wives invariably are that way because of what's on the inside rather than what's offered to them from the outside.

Money, power, and prestige are not what make Daniel tick. Daniel refused to interpret the sign for remuneration. Yet he did interpret the sign for Belshazzar. Why? Why did he comply with the king's request, especially since the writing on the wall foretold of the king's imminent demise (vv. 26–28)? The text does not answer this question explicitly, however, I do have a theory: Daniel chose to interpret the sign without compensation simply because it was his job. Allow me to unpack this thought some more.

At the beginning of the book we are told that Daniel was among the Jewish youth who, because of their intellectual prowess, had been chosen by King Nebuchadnezzar to be trained for his royal service (1:3–5). Further, we are told that this "knowledge and understanding of all kinds of literature and learning" possessed by Daniel and his three friends had been given to them by God (1:17), and because the foursome had been gifted by God with surpassing intellectual abilities, the king eventually summoned them to his service, where Daniel remained, serving as a member of the royal court, all the way into the reign of the Persian King Cyrus (1:19–21). At the end of chapter 2 we are told that Daniel's ability to recall and interpret

---

3. Kohn, "Incentive Plans" (emphasis original).

Nebuchadnezzar's dream led to his promotion to a high position in the kingdom, and because he had secured the king's ear, he helped to promote his friends Shadrach, Meshach, and Abednego (2:48). When the queen describes Daniel in the fifth chapter, she mentions that King Nebuchadnezzar had appointed him chief of the magicians, enchanters, astrologers, and diviners because of Daniel's fantastic wisdom and intelligence (5:11).

Thus, God had specifically gifted and equipped Daniel to serve in the king's court. It was God's plan for Daniel to spend his life counselling the foreign kings whom God sovereignly raised up to rule over his people Israel. How committed was Daniel to this vocational calling of his? Consider this: Daniel's final revelation came in the third year of King Cyrus (10:1), but according to Ezra 1:1–4, Cyrus ordered the release of the Jewish exiles so that they could return to the Promised Land and rebuild Jerusalem during the *first* year of his reign. That means that Daniel chose to remain in Babylonia rather than return to the land of Israel with his people. God had sovereignly chosen Daniel and placed him in this position of influence in the royal court. I believe Daniel knew this, and that's why he could perform at the high level he did. By serving the king, he was serving God. "Whatever you do, work at it with all your heart, as working for the Lord, not for human masters." I believe Daniel's obedient service to Belshazzar was tied to a personal sense of divine calling. That sense of vocational calling is what made Daniel tick and what drove him to perform his duties with surpassing distinction.

As believers today living in social and cultural exile, it's vital that we follow Daniel's example and serve God through our on-the-job excellence. I greatly enjoyed my graduate studies at McMaster University. Because I did my PhD in the Religious Studies Department of a secular institution of higher learning, our department had many students as well as faculty who did not hold any faith commitments to Christianity. So, I often found our times of interaction stimulating and rich. In my first year I quickly became friends with a fellow believer who was in his final year. He was a godly young man whose stellar academic reputation preceded him. In many ways he became the gold standard by which the rest of us in the program came to be measured. I can still remember one of my fellow students complaining to me about how poorly his advisory committee meeting had just gone (which actually was kind of the norm for all of us), and how unfair it was that he was expected to perform at my Christian friend's high level of achievement. I found that comment fascinating because this student didn't know my friend, nor had he even met him, yet he clearly knew of his sterling academic record. That's part of what it means to follow Daniel's example: to serve God with distinction wherever he plants us.

Often, *serving with distinction comes through a sense of divine calling*, i.e., a conviction that God has appointed you to a specific place in order to serve his purposes there, and so bring honor to his name. Martin Luther King Jr. said it this way:

> If a man *is called* to be a street sweeper, he should sweep streets even as Michelangelo painted or Beethoven composed or Shakespeare wrote. He should sweep streets so well that all of the host of heaven and earth will pause to say, "Here lived a great street sweeper who did his job well!"[4]

The reason a street sweeper can sweep streets with such distinction is because he knows that he has been called by God to this vocation. Ultimately, then, he knows that he sweeps streets not for remuneration or fear of reprisal (should he not sweep), but to the glory of God.

I also believe it was Daniel's passion for God's glory that, ironically, kept him out of sight during his friends' run-in with Nebuchadnezzar back in chapter 3. Remember the scene: Nebuchadnezzar had built a massive statue of gold on the plain of Dura and commanded all the people of his kingdom to worship it. The story centered around Shadrach, Meshach, and Abednego's refusal to comply with the king's edict, and their consequent sentencing to the incinerator. The question I initially raised in chapter 3 was: where was Daniel in all of this? I believe that Daniel had previously been dispatched by Nebuchadnezzar to another part of the Babylonian Empire to attend to some important affairs for the throne; he was, after all, as we've read, a renowned problem solver. Therefore, he was not with his friends during this time, nor even in that part of the vast kingdom. However, given the enormity and peculiarity of the statue's construction, Daniel would probably have received word about it, and his reaction would almost certainly have been the same as his friends'. If all of this is right, then the question now becomes, why did Daniel, upon hearing of the statue's construction, not curtail his business trip and protest the king's edict alongside of Shadrach, Meshach, and Abednego?

If what I've said is correct, viz., that Daniel served his king out of a sense of divine calling, then the reason Daniel did not return to protest

---

4. King, "Three Dimensions."

is because he believed that he could best serve God by staying put and fulfilling the obligations of his royal appointment. Daniel recognized that, ultimately, it was God who had appointed him (having so specifically gifted and equipped him) to rule over the province. While it would not have necessarily been wrong for Daniel to cut his trip short to join his friends, neither would it have necessarily been wise. Daniel's presence was obviously not needed for his friends' deliverance and consequent witness to Nebuchadnezzar. His presence, however, was more likely needed where he was in order to accomplish the task(s) for which the king had dispatched him; and in completing the king's business, his esteemed reputation as a gifted problem solver continued to grow. Consequently, Daniel glorified God.

For a truly Christian witness, excellence cannot go it alone. By itself excellence can breed elitism and condescension. We all know or have met people who are tremendous at what they do, but we can't stand being around them because they're so full of themselves. We find these people in our workplace, in our neighbouhood, in our school, on our team, in our church, on social media—they're everywhere. All that giftedness, all that greatness, yet we still try our best to spend as little time with them as possible. Why? Excellence by itself is often insufferable because of the underlying negative attitudes and behaviors that often accompany it.

But when it works in concert with other virtues (like compassion—see the previous chapter) as it did with Daniel, then excellence has more of a magnetic affect on people. We routinely witness this effect in politics. Voters want more than just competence from their candidates. We want someone we can identify with. We are less likely to vote for someone who we think can't relate to our way of life. In the tidal wave of analysis that took place in the aftermath of the 2012 US presidential election, numerous pundits concluded that one of the things that hurt Mitt Romney's campaign was the way he often came across to voters. Many people perceived him as lacking empathy with "ordinary folks." Conversely, one of the things that helped George W. Bush and Bill Clinton win their two elections was their "one of the boys" persona: they came across as extremely down-to-earth, and much easier to relate to than either of their campaign counterparts.

Excellence by itself has the ability to repel people. Paul put it like this: "[If I] can fathom all mysteries and all knowledge, and if I have a faith that can move mountains, but do not have love, I am nothing" (1 Cor 13:2). Excellence must be accompanied by mercy and love and other virtues if it is to speak powerfully to our society, especially when our collective voice as Christians comes from the margins.

But although excellence by itself has the potential to repel, mediocrity not only repels it attracts ridicule. The exilic church, as it tends to the business of God's kingdom, cannot afford to be mediocre. I don't like musicals—there, I said it. I just think there's too much singing in musicals, that's all. One of the most famous and beloved musicals of all time (or so I'm told) is *The Sound of Music*. Ordinarily, I would never watch a movie like that, regardless of all the awards and all the accolades it has received. The only reason I did watch it once, back in the 90s, was because I was in love, and I was pursuing the girl of my dreams (who, thankfully, is now my wife). She loved the movie and wanted me to watch it with her. Well, what's a guy to do? I watched it. Did I like it? No (although the shooting part and the chase scene were pretty cool). And I still don't like musicals. But I certainly recognized the more-than-immense skills and abilities that went into producing that movie. The film was done exceedingly well, and I can appreciate that.

Much of our society today doesn't like what the church is about. We get up early on Sundays—rather than enjoy the pleasure of sleeping in—to gather together to sing songs, quietly listen to someone speak to us for half an hour (sometimes more), and give a percentage of our modest, hard-earned, heavily taxed income to finance church operations. During the week we might even return to the church in order to sit quietly and pray with other people for about an hour. Can you see why some people might be turned off by this routine, especially if all of this is done poorly? However, if we serve with clear and obvious distinction, yes, some people still will not like the church, but at the very least they will have to recognize the excellence with which we serve and honor our God.

The exilic church must be about the Lord's business in such a way that, when our "captors" observe how well we accomplish our King's assigned duties, they still might not like us, but they will have to respect us, and in so doing they "will praise [our] Father in heaven" (Matt 5:16b; CEV).

Questions for Further Reflection

1. Why does excellence bring more glory to God than mediocrity? Is there anything at which you excel or would like to excel? How can you use your excellence to bring glory to God?

2. Does excellence in and of itself glorify God? How can you guard against becoming prideful in your abilities?

3. Do you feel a sense of divine calling to your current vocation? Should you? Why or why not? How does a sense of calling affect job performance?

4. What does an excellent local church look like? What does a mediocre church look like? Can an excellent church become mediocre? How?

5. How can a local church function with excellence within the broader, non-Christian community?

6

Embracing Integrity

I know, my God, that you test the heart and are pleased with integrity.
—1 CHR 29:17A

ALTHOUGH WIDELY HELD THAT a huge tear in its hull from an iceberg sank the Titanic on its maiden voyage in 1912, a 1997 *New York Times* article reported that a group of scientists believed a series of slits was what actually downed the luxurious 900-foot cruise liner in one of the worst maritime disasters of all time. According to the article, an international team of divers and scientists examined the wreckage, buried two and a half miles below the surface under the ocean mire, using sound wave technology. The team discovered that the damage, far from being some enormous three-hundred-foot gash, simply consisted of six narrow slits across the six watertight holds. Those tiny slits had compromised the structural integrity of the hull, causing the magnificent vessel to sink.[1] Sometime it's the "small knife" that cuts the deepest. Not only do tiny tears have the potential to bring down a grand ship, they can sink a great reputation.

Daniel's reputation for excellence followed him even into the reign of the Persians, who succeeded the Babylonians: "Now Daniel so distinguished himself among the administrators and the satraps by his exceptional qualities that the king planned to set him over the whole kingdom" (6:3). The NIV speaks of Daniel's "exceptional qualities"—"qualities" being

---

1. Broad, "Toppling Theories."

plural. It wasn't just his on-the-job excellence that separated Daniel from the rest of the political pack; there were other qualities. Doubtless, some of these qualities we have already discussed: his humility, commitment, and caring spirit. Another important quality is showcased in this section of the story: Daniel's integrity.

The Bible speaks a fair bit about integrity. We are explicitly told, for example, that Job (Job 2:3), David (Ps 78:72), and Jesus (Matt 22:16) were men of integrity. *The Concise Oxford Dictionary* defines integrity as "wholeness" or "soundness." The idea behind integrity is not mere consistency but a uniformity or seamlessness in a person's character. While integrity does not mean an absence of chips in a person's character, it does mean that there are no deep, fundamental flaws or fissures that have the potential to rupture and ruin an otherwise good character. I believe integrity consists of two parts: a positive component, viz., what someone does, and a negative component, what someone does not do. We see both of these at work in Daniel.

In chapter 6, Daniel displays integrity's negative component first. Upon hearing that King Darius planned to elevate Daniel above all the other administrators,

> [T]he administrators and the satraps tried to find grounds for charges against Daniel in his conduct of government affairs, but they were unable to do so. They could find no corruption in him, because he was trustworthy and neither corrupt nor negligent. Finally these men said, "We will never find any basis for charges against this man Daniel unless it has something to do with the law of his God." (vv. 4–5)

Integrity manifests in what a person does not do. In other words, it is expressed in the activities and behaviours from which someone refrains. In Daniel's case, he did not engage in corrupt practices. The jealous administrators searched for skeletons in Daniel's closet so that they could oust him from the royal court, but they found none. You get the impression from the text that this went on for quite some time. Finally, they resorted to a scheme based on something that most obviously marked Daniel: his commitment to God.

The administrators knew that Daniel expressed his commitment to God through a steadfast prayer life, so they tricked King Darius into passing a law whereby any person who prayed to someone other than the king for a thirty-day period would be thrown to the lions. At this point in the narrative Daniel demonstrates the positive component of integrity:

> Now when Daniel learned that the decree had been published, he went home to his upstairs room where the windows opened toward Jerusalem. Three times a day he got down on his knees and prayed, giving thanks to his God, just as he had done before. (v. 10)

Beyond simply manifesting in what a person does not do, *integrity manifests in what a person does do*. In other words, it is conveyed by the activities and behaviours in which someone does engage. Daniel continued to pray to God despite the royal prohibition.

Integrity gets tested in two domains. Firstly, it gets tested publicly. Daniel would have been tempted to compromise himself in the public sphere. That's because temptations can come from without, from the outside. Given the dubious character of the royal administrators, not only did they search for skeletons of corruption in Daniel's closet, I would imagine that they also tried to plant some skeletons of their own. In other words, they probably tried to set up Daniel, perhaps with a bribery scheme. People in power often take bribes. I would bet that some of these guys had probably taken a kickback or two—so why not Daniel? But since they ended up having to resort to a bogus prayer ban, obviously any such bribery plot had failed. And why would it have failed? Because only a person driven by power, pleasure, and/or materialism is susceptible to bribery. That's why the person takes the bribe in the first place: to get more money or more pleasure or to feel a greater sense of power. But as we saw previously, Daniel was not like that. He was not into personal gain or glory. Remember his reply to the king in chapter 5? "You may keep your gifts for yourself and give your rewards to someone else" (5:17a). Daniel's excellence operated independently of any desire for personal gain. He performed at a high level of achievement because, ultimately, he knew he was working for God and for his glory, not for the sake of reward. It's kind of hard to bribe someone like that.

Temptations can come from without, and sometimes without warning. At one of my former churches, one of my parishioners, knowing I had three young kids, offered me some children's DVD movies he had. I didn't recognize the titles but I accepted them anyway. When I got home and showed them to my wife, she promptly informed me that two of the movies had only just finished their runs in the theatre while the third was still playing. I promptly returned the movies for two reasons. First, they were illegal. But my second reason was this: the church had had serious leadership issues in its recent past; because I was still new at the church and did not yet know this gentleman, the thought had occurred to me that he might be testing me or setting me up. Although I later learned this was not the case, nowadays you can never be too careful.

Not only was Daniel's integrity tested in the public realm, it was also tested privately; temptations can come from within. The temptation for Daniel would have been not to pray. After all, who would know? And it would have been very easy for him to rationalize his prayer stoppage, wouldn't it? "It's only for thirty days. What's thirty days? After the ban expires I'll make it up by praying six times a day!" Or, rather than cease from praying altogether, Daniel could have changed the way he prayed: instead of always praying in front of his upstairs window, he could have prayed in a closet (or under his bed). "What difference does it make where I pray so long as I pray, right? Who's going to know?"

You don't need someone offering you a bribe in order to be tempted to compromise your integrity. Some jobs have their own built-in temptations that other jobs don't. As a pastor, I (like many other pastors) had a "hospitality" account—basically an expense account to use at my discretion. Typically, I used it when treating members of the church to coffee or to a meal. The temptation for me here was to misuse this expense account—to eat at places I normally would not, to order courses I normally would not, to expense items that really shouldn't be expensed. Thankfully, I did not succumb to these temptations, but I know of pastors who have (and members of the Canadian Senate, to boot!). Temptations can come from within. James recognized this when he wrote that "each person is tempted when they are dragged away by their own evil desire and enticed" (Jas 1:14).

Temptation to compromise can be particularly strong in circumstances of anonymity. When we are with people who do not know that we are Christian or who have no prior history with us, it can be tempting to let our witness slide—"After all, no one knows who I am or what I am about?" That's exactly what I thought when I left home to go to college. While living in the dorms in my first year, I began to develop some very bad habits. I began swearing; and not just a little, but a lot—enough to make a sailor blush. But hey, since I essentially didn't have a past with these guys, I was safe, so to speak, because nobody knew that I normally didn't swear. And besides, if I swore it was okay because everybody else did. I also began looking at pornography. Here again, because my dorm mates didn't know that I was a Christian, I was safe; and besides, I wasn't doing anything that everyone else wasn't already doing. But here's the thing with integrity (which I obviously did not have at the time): it operates regardless of the audience. Integrity perseveres regardless of who is or isn't watching, as *National Post* columnist Jeff Jedras put it: "[Ethics] is how you act when no one is looking."[2] The psalmist wrote, "I will be careful to lead a blameless life—when will you come to me? I will conduct the affairs of my house with a blameless heart. I will not look with approval on anything that is vile" (101:2–3a). The writer of this psalm was deeply concerned to live righteously—not just publicly but privately, in the confines of his own home (in his own room).

Remember the Oxford Dictionary's definition of integrity? "Wholeness." Well, the wholeness of integrity produces a consistent life. Thus, besides manifesting in what a person does or does not do, *integrity produces a consistent or seamless life.* Daniel was consistent. Daniel could have ceased praying for thirty days. He could have prayed in a more secluded area of his home. Or he could have responded to the royal edict in a more confrontational, in-your-face manner, similar to his friends' response to Nebuchadnezzar in chapter 3. He could have, for example, rebuked the king for this new ban that flouted God's law, and Daniel could have openly flouted the royal edict by praying right outside the king's palace. But none of these options would have been consistent with Daniel's character or his personality. Daniel's response to the decree not only fit seamlessly with God's law, but also with who Daniel was as a person. You could say that in this way Daniel was being authentic.

The exilic church needs desperately to become an authentic church. The business world has started to discover its own need for authenticity. The May 28, 2008, edition of *Bloomberg Businessweek* published a perceptive article, "How to Stand Out? Try Authenticity," by Sohrab Vossoughi, the founder and president of ZIBA Design. On a weekly basis, high-level executives ask Vossoughi how they can differentiate their company in the marketplace, to which he responds, "Forget different. Try authentic." Vossoughi suggests that authenticity is crucial in the twenty-first century because the public has generally come to distrust businesses and institutions, because media-savvy consumers can more easily spot insincerity, and because reality TV and online personas have caused consumers to adopt something of a hermeneutics of suspicion (my term), needing frequently

2. Jedras, "Strahl Needs to Learn."

to ask, is this genuinely real or simply staged "reality"? According to Vossoughi, "Consumers seek meaning and a brand they can trust."³

I believe these observations have clear relevance for the Western church in the twenty-first century. For decades churches have tried to mimic the world by offering people experiences they can find in the world in terms of music, entertainment, or physical aesthetics. For years churches have sought to become more "consumer friendly" by packaging the gospel such that its message doesn't sound quite so foreign, strange, or disturbing. But for all of our striving to operate according to the "good" that we can see in the world, we have failed to recognize that people want meaning and someone they can trust. Society seeks authenticity, not production. The exilic church needs to lead the way in authenticity, not fall behind.

In addition to giving us a window into Daniel's integrity, chapter 6 also offers us a brief but helpful glimpse into how Daniel prayed during the prohibition. We are told first that Daniel "prayed, giving thanks to his God" (v. 10b). Daniel prayed giving thanks—but for what? An edict had just been issued that said that anyone caught praying to any god other than the king will be sentenced to the lions' den, and Daniel offered thanksgiving to God? Is this guy for real? Actually, he's probably about as real as Paul and Silas. When they were preaching in Philippi, they were set upon by an angry crowd, stripped, severely flogged, and thrown into the inner cell of a prison with their feet in stocks (Acts 16:19–25). Such harsh treatment would make most people whimper and curl up into the fetal position (if not for those darn stocks). Paul and Silas, however, pulled a "Daniel": "About midnight Paul and Silas were praying and singing hymns to God, and the other prisoners were listening to them" (Acts 16:25). I bet I can guess what the other prisoners were saying to each other: "Are these guys for real?" About as real as Daniel.

We don't exactly know what Daniel was thanking God for; we can only speculate. But I feel pretty certain, especially given the whole tone of the story, that one of the things Daniel thanked God for was his sovereignty. The same God who sent the Israelites into exile, who oversaw the destruction of Jerusalem and the temple where his name had dwelt, who spoke to a pagan king to show him the future of the nations, is completely sovereign over the affairs of all people, big and small; and even now, he permitted this deadly prayer ban dilemma to arise. Remember the words of Nebuchadnezzar the convert, "He does as he pleases with the powers of heaven and the

---

3. Vossoughi, "How to Stand Out?"

peoples of the earth" (4:35). God was not wringing his hands over Daniel's perilous predicament. He was still in control of what was going on. Daniel believed that, so he thanked God.

Second, we read that when the royal administrators found Daniel, he was "praying and asking God for help" (v. 11b). Just because Daniel believed God was sovereign didn't mean that he was a fatalist, i.e., believing that whatever happens happens, and there's nothing anyone can do but sit back and let it happen. Nor was Daniel's faith the "in the sweet by and by" kind, where his prayer involved nothing but praise. Daniel thanked God but, because of his difficult circumstances, he also asked God for his help. In this way, Daniel was very much a realist. His situation was dire. He needed help so he turned to his God and requested his assistance. The text does not say if Daniel specified in his petition the form of aid God should send. In other words, did Daniel pray that no one would find out that he had been violating the prohibition? Did he ask God that the king would somehow rescind his decree, or that he could find a loophole through which he could escape? Did he pray for the grace to endure his fate courageously? Or did he ask God to make the lions vegetarians? We don't know for sure. In keeping with the notion of God's sovereignty, he may very well have just prayed for help generally and then trusted God to fill in the details of what form his provision should take.

The rest of the story details how God answered Daniel's cry for help. When Daniel was caught praying, the king gave the order for him to be thrown into the lions' den. The next morning when the king went to the den to check on Daniel's condition, "Daniel answered, 'May the king live forever! My God sent his angel, and he shut the mouths of the lions. They have not hurt me'" (vv. 21–22a). God answered Daniel's prayer for help through a remarkable, angelic intervention. But it was King Darius's behaviour in all of this that is more pertinent to our study. His reaction shows that *integrity bears fruit with people.*

Through the first half of the chapter, we are given little indication that Darius was any different than his predecessor, Belshazzar. That initial impression, however, changes dramatically. When the administrators revealed to the king that Daniel had been defying the royal edict, "he was greatly distressed; he was determined to rescue Daniel and made every effort until sundown to save him" (v. 14). The king obviously realized the foolishness of his hasty decree: because of it, his otherwise exceptional administrator, whom he was about to establish as ruler over the entire kingdom, had been set up by the other (very jealous) court administrators, duping him into ordering Daniel's execution. Later we read that after Darius gave the order, he "spent the night without eating and without any entertainment being brought to him. And he could not sleep" (v. 18). Not only was the king absolutely miserable because of Daniel's situation, but he was haunted by it: as he lay on his bed, sleep evaded him. His misery was not simply driven by guilt but by a profound concern for his top aide's well-being. That is why at the crack of down the king got up and "hurried to the lions' den" (v. 19b). Daniel's innocence in the matter was proven by the lions' inability to hurt him. Consequently, the king had his accusers thrown into the den, whereupon the lions instantly "overpowered them and crushed all their bones" (v. 24b).

All of this leads me to believe that Daniel had been a powerful positive witness to Darius. The king greatly respected and admired Daniel not simply for his on-the-job excellence but, moreover, he respected and admired his integrity: twice the king referred to Daniel as the one who *continually* served his God (vv. 16, 20). Daniel's commitment to God, as far as the king could see, was characterized by a seamless consistency: his lifestyle was wholly predicated on serving the God of Israel. This steadfast commitment did not allow Daniel to stop praying—not even for thirty days. Because Daniel served God with integrity, he had integrity with people, like with Darius. Consequently, King Darius issued a new decree whereby all the people of his kingdom "must fear and reverence the God of Daniel" (v. 26b). Integrity bears fruit: it makes a positive impact on those around us.

One of society's legitimate beefs with the church is our lack of integrity. In a February 2012 post on his blog, "The Palmer Perspective," Christian pastor and author Sean Palmer asked the question, "Does Your Congregation Lead with Integrity?" He had recently had four conversations with lay leaders serving in different local churches from around the country. All four voiced the same concern about their congregation: a lack of integrity. One person, to his dismay, discovered while serving as the church accountant that only the senior pastor and one of the elders tithed—out of a total of twelve elders and staff. Another person felt like she was being robbed because, although the staff at her church kept an hourly log of time and work, it became increasingly clear that the singles' pastor rarely worked more than twenty hours a week, yet was being paid for forty. A husband and wife at another church bemoaned the fact that their leadership regularly skirted around legal requirements and paid contractors under the table. Still another lamented that when their preacher left in the midst of a sex scandal, rather than informing the congregation what happened for the sake of clarity and closure, the leaders sought to cover it up. Palmer concluded that in each instance the integrity of a church was at stake, and therefore he calls for a "ferocious commitment to integrity," for a lack of integrity costs us our credibility.[4] A person without integrity can never be trusted; and if they cannot be trusted then, whenever they have something valuable to say, they will not be heard but ignored. Could it be that one of the factors that led to the Western church's exile to the margins was its lack of integrity?

Asaph testified how "David shepherded [Israel] with integrity of heart" (Ps 78:72a). Doubtless there were times that it was clear to the people of Israel that King David led them with integrity (and probably times they knew otherwise). But sometimes the integrity move will go unnoticed. Nobody will ever know about the financial sacrifice made for integrity's sake; no one will ever understand the marital strain endured in order to help out someone in need; most will never appreciate having to delay long-desired study or publishing plans for the sake of shepherding the flock. But integrity will sometimes demand that we make that difficult choice, as David declared, "I know, my God, that you test the heart and are pleased with integrity" (1 Chr 29:17a). Thankfully, although some of our integrity moves will remain unseen by most, God sees them all. He understands and he appreciates them: "[Y]our Father, who sees what is done in secret, will reward you" (Matt 6:4, 6, 18).

In the end, Daniel's integrity saved him from the lions: "They have not hurt me, because I was found innocent in his sight. Nor have I ever done any wrong before you, Your Majesty" (v. 22). And yet, what if God in his sovereignty had allowed Daniel to die in the lions' den? Would that have affected his witness to Darius? I don't think so. His death simply would have made him a martyr. Earlier, Shadrach, Meshach, and Abednego were prepared for martyrdom; surely Daniel would have been too. And while martyrdom is the final word in one sense (i.e., the end of the physical life of the witness), in another sense it offers a fresh word, for "by faith [the martyr] still speaks even though he is dead" (Heb 11:4b). The life message of the witness continues in and even after death.

---

4. Palmer, "Does Your Congregation Lead with Integrity?"

Embracing Integrity

"I know, my God, that you test the heart and are pleased with integrity." David was actually only partly right: God is pleased with integrity . . . but so are people.

Questions for Further Reflection

1. If you were in Daniel's shoes regarding the ban on prayer, what would you have done? Explain why.

2. What is it about integrity that impresses people? What are some ways that you model integrity publicly? How about privately? Are there temptations to compromise your integrity? Are there steps you can take to prevent this from happening?

3. What does it mean to live authentically? What hinders you from living this way?

4. What are some ways that local congregations can become more authentic in their dealings with each other? How about in their dealings with the broader, non-Christian community?

5. How can the local church model integrity to outsiders?

Part 2

God's Message for His Community

7

God Is Infinitely Great

Great is the Lord and most worthy of praise; his greatness no one can fathom.

—PS 145:3

THE FINDINGS OF A 2005 study commissioned by the British Cheese Board showed that different varieties of cheese can induce certain types of dreams. In the study, two hundred volunteers ate twenty grams of cheese thirty minutes before going to sleep, and then reported on the nature of their dreams. Eighty percent of those who ate Stilton cheese had surreal dreams about vegetarian crocodiles, soldiers using kittens as weapons, and a dinner party where the guests were camels. Those who ate Lancashire cheese tended to dream about the future. Sixty percent of those who ate Leicester dreamt of past events from their childhood. Many who ate Cheshire cheese couldn't recall their dreams, while Cheddar cheese seemed to induce dreams involving celebrities; one girl helped to form a human pyramid under the tutelage of Johnny Depp. Apparently, sweet dreams are made of cheese. Who am I to disagree?

The first half of the book of Daniel presents us with lessons on how to live during the Western church's social and cultural exile. As we follow Daniel's example of commitment, caring, excellence, and integrity, we will offer a wise witness to our hostile society. As mentioned earlier, chapters 5–9 are mixed up chronologically. According to the references to the specific reigns cited, the chronological order of these chapters is actually 7, 8, 5, 9, 6. As we saw in chapter 5, one of the reasons for the canonical order has more to do with character contrasts (Belshazzar vs. Nebuchadnezzar) than with historical chronology. The second half of Daniel deals with the dreams and visions God gave Daniel about the future of his people and their oppressors. These were messages God knew people needed to hear in order to offer them instruction and encouragement, rebuke and reassurance, coaching and comfort.

A Word about Dreams

Before we turn to the substance of the first oracle, I think it would be worthwhile to discuss briefly the strange and symbolic character of dreams and visions. If you've already read Daniel or some other parts of the Bible (e.g., Revelation), you have no doubt noticed the highly symbolic and often hard to understand medium of dreams and visions. Even God's own prophets at times needed to be spoon-fed the interpretation (like Daniel). If God wants us to know what he's saying, why does he make it so difficult? Now, to be fair, God doesn't always speak in *New York Times* crossword-puzzle-like messages. In fact, most of his Word seems pretty plain. And when he speaks to us in the moment through his "still, small voice," we usually don't need to lock ourselves up in a room with a concordance and a commentary for three days to decipher his message. We usually know what he's telling us in that moment (whether or not we obey is another issue). But yet, there are other times when he chooses to speak through highly symbolic dreams or visions whose meanings are far from self-evident. If, for example, God wanted to speak to Daniel in a dream about the succession of kingdoms, why didn't he simply verbalize it in the dream: "Daniel, there is going to be a succession of kingdoms, yada, yada, yada . . ."? Or better yet, forget the dream altogether, why not just say it using direct propositions in an audible voice?

I think there are at least three reasons why God chooses the language of dreams and visions. First, symbols are more memorable than propositional statements. How easy we forget what someone has just said five minutes ago (okay, maybe that's just me), yet we are able to remember dreams we had *years* ago. Memory plays a valuable role in our faith. In some ways, our faith in God is only as strong as our memory. That is why, for example, the risen Christ urged the church in Ephesus, "Consider how far you have fallen! Repent and do the things you did at first" (Rev 2:5). Remembering would help the church to repent and live with a renewed passion for Jesus.

We also see the vital role memory plays for faith when the Israelites were preparing to enter the Promised Land. Moses repeatedly urged the people (some twenty times throughout the book of Deuteronomy) to "remember" God and "not to forget" everything the Lord had done for them in bringing them out of Egypt, so that they would not forsake him:

> When you have eaten and are satisfied, praise the LORD your God for the good land he has given you. Be careful that you do not forget the LORD your God. . . . You may say to yourself, "My power and the strength of my hands have produced this wealth for me." But remember the LORD your God, for it is he who gives you the ability to produce wealth. (Deut 8:10–11a, 17–18a)

Unfortunately for Israel, they eventually forgot . . . and they fell away. By speaking in highly symbolic language, I believe God actually makes it easier for us to remember and recall his messages, and by so doing, strengthen our faith in him.

A second reason God communicates through the symbolically charged language of dreams and visions is to humble us. I believe he accomplishes this in two ways. On the one hand, symbolic language possesses a mystery that elicits awe and wonder that mere statements cannot. Mystery has this effect because it implies a lack of knowledge on our part and, consequently, imparts a sense of powerlessness—because we can't figure it out—making us immediately aware of our own limitations. In other words, the meaning of a symbol is at first incomprehensible to us and beyond our understanding. To come face to face with our own limitations is a humbling experience.

On the other hand, when we don't understand a dream's meaning we have to ask God for help; and asking another for help—even if it's God—is always humbling. And that's precisely what God wants to do: he wants to humble us. And while there are a number of reasons why God seeks to humble us, perhaps the most significant reason is so that we might become more like his Son Jesus: "In your relationships with one another, have the same mindset as Christ Jesus: who . . . taking the very nature of a servant . . . he humbled himself" (Phil 2:5–8).

The third reason God sometimes communicates through the metaphor of dreams and visions is this: even though God desires to humble us and have us ask him for help to interpret his coded messages, he also wants to engage our minds. Now at first, this might seem like an odd way to engage our minds; after all, isn't that what mathematics, chemistry, and physics are for? I took those courses in high school and college and I don't remember there being strange, symbolic language that needed special deciphering (other than maybe the questions I couldn't answer). So, how are our minds engaged?

At different times we can actually spot a mentally engaged Daniel trying to make sense of what he has seen in a dream. For example, after his dream of the four beasts Daniel said, "I, Daniel, was troubled in spirit, and the visions that passed through my mind disturbed me. I approached one of those standing there and asked him the meaning of all this" (7:15–16). Daniel was disturbed by the dream and couldn't understand its meaning, so he asked for help. On another occasion, as he watched the initial stages of a vision of a wild, charging ram, the text says that Daniel "was thinking about this" (8:5a). The Hebrew word for "thinking about" appears frequently throughout the Old Testament. For example, it occurs more than thirty times just in the book of Proverbs, where it is frequently associated with terms like "learning," "knowledge," and "understanding." Daniel was trying to decipher the meaning of what he just saw. As the vision came to a completion, we read that he was "watching the vision and trying to understand it" (8:15). Since, however, he came up short of the interpretation, God said, "Gabriel, tell this man the meaning of the vision" (8:16).

There are times when Daniel seems to understand the symbolism immediately with little thought (e.g., in 4:19), but other times he cannot. In these instances his mind actively seeks to understand the message but the meaning comes only through God's direct or indirect (i.e., angelic) intervention. The point is that Daniel's mind is sometimes deeply engaged in the activity of dream/vision interpretation. Not only does memory play a crucial role in our faith, but so does our mind. Jesus declares that the greatest commandment is to "Love the Lord your God with all your heart and with all our soul and with all your mind" (Matt 22:37). The Apostle Paul, in beginning to explain the gospel to the Roman church, declares that while human beings have been given over to a depraved mind (Rom 1:28), because of God's gracious act of salvation, Christians can now be transformed into the image of Christ through the renewing of their minds (Rom 12:2).

Daniel's "mindful" experience is actually not that unique. We are told that what set Moses apart from the prophets that would follow him was the direct way in which God spoke to him. With the subsequent prophets,

God would reveal himself in visions and "speak to them in dreams" (Num 12:6b); but not so with Moses: with him God spoke "face to face, clearly and not in riddles" (Num 12:8a). The comparison here is telling: not only could God's prophets periodically speak in riddles, but God communicated to his own prophets in riddles! And we all know that a good riddle is something that a person must work at in order to understand and solve. So, through dreams (and visions) God speaks memorably in order to humble people and to engage their minds.

Daniel's First Message

Regarding the second half of the book, God spoke to Daniel through dreams and visions, not to satisfy some sweet tooth for the supernatural he might have had, but to give him powerful words of encouragement to pass on to others. There is a fair bit of overlap between the series of visions in chapters 7–12 and their meanings. Nevertheless, I believe each one offers a slightly different word of consolation and instruction for Daniel's audience. If chapter 1 functions as the introduction to the entire book, then I would say that chapter 7, the first of Daniel's visions, sets the tone for the rest of this section of the book. I believe the thrust of this first dream is this: *God is infinitely great.*

The dream Daniel receives in chapter 7 takes place "in the first year of Belshazzar" (v. 1a). Daniel's dream of the four beasts mirrors the dream that God gave Nebuchadnezzar years earlier (ch. 2), except the successive kingdoms are now represented by beasts rather than by the parts of a statue. In Daniel's dream, God revealed the succession of kingdoms that will take place in the future: the lion represents Babylonia; the bear the Medo-Persian Empire; the leopard the Greek Empire, followed by a fourth, terrifying beast, which represents the Roman Empire. While it is this kind of far-reaching prophetic pronouncement that led Christian translators of the Bible to place the book of Daniel among the so-called Major Prophets (i.e., alongside of Isaiah, Jeremiah, and Ezekiel), I wish to focus on other aspects of God's message to his servant in this chapter.

In the dream Daniel is given a vision of God's throne, whereby God reveals to him something of his infinite greatness:

> As I looked, thrones were set in place, and the Ancient of Days took his seat. His clothing was as white as snow; the hair of his head was white like wool. His throne was flaming with fire, and

> its wheels were all ablaze. A river of fire was flowing, coming out from before him. Thousands upon thousands attended him; ten thousand times ten thousand stood before him. The court was seated, and the books were opened. (vv. 9–10)

God's infinite greatness is revealed by his supreme kingship. The first things Daniel noticed are thrones; and among these thrones God takes his seat upon his own unique throne. The thrones Daniel saw were probably angelic thrones, similar to John's vision in Revelation: "Surrounding [God's] throne were twenty-four other thrones, and seated on them were twenty-four elders. They were dressed in white and had crowns of gold on their heads" (Rev 4:4). Above the kings of the world exist mightier, angelic kings, and above even these heavenly monarchs is God. Paul echoes this sentiment when he writes, "[Christ is seated] in the heavenly realms, far above all rule and authority, power and dominion, and every title that can be given, not only in the present age but also in the one to come" (Eph 1:20b–21).

The fiery nature of God's throne also depicts the supremacy of his kingship: it is "flaming with fire," its wheels were "all ablaze," and a "river of fire" was flowing from it. Fire often symbolizes the manifest presence of God. For example, God appeared to Moses in a burning bush that somehow resisted being consumed in the flames (Exod 3:2–3). Fire can also represent divine holiness or moral purity: the prophet Malachi declared that the Lord's coming would be like "a refiner's fire" so as to purify his people (Mal 3:2). God's presence and his purity are interwoven. When Moses approached the burning bush, God warned him, "Do not come any closer. . . . Take off your sandals, for the place where you are standing is holy ground" (Exod 3:5). God's throne, then, remains wholly untainted and absolutely free of any stain or hint of sin or corruption.

What I find particularly striking in this vision is that God's throne has wheels: "its wheels were all ablaze." In all of the pictures of monarchs' thrones, I've yet to come across one with wheels. I think the significance of the wheels becomes apparent when we recall the story's exilic setting. Remember the dilemma for Diaspora Jews: God had promised in the days of Solomon to fill the Jerusalem temple with his presence; but what about Jews who lived beyond the borders of Jerusalem? Would God still be with them? Many Jews believed that the omnipresent God of the Jews dwelt in Jerusalem in a special way that he did not dwell elsewhere. Hence, even Daniel faced Jerusalem to pray (6:10a). Nevertheless, Jewish believers could still count on God to be with them even outside the holy city. The

God Is Infinitely Great

blazing wheels symbolize the mobility of God's throne: God is able to move wherever his people go. This vision of a "mobile God" finds a close parallel in the exilic prophet Ezekiel's vision in the opening chapter of his prophecy. No Jew, then, is so far from Jerusalem that s/he is beyond reach of God and his sovereign rule.

God's expansive kingship is reflected in the number of his attendants. The White House's 2012 Annual Report to Congress reported 468 employees in its fold, working ultimately for its chief resident, President Barack Obama. According to the British Monarchy website, the royal household employs 1,200 people to support Queen Elizabeth II. Daniel observed that God's royal attendants number "thousands upon thousands" and "ten thousand times ten thousand," which is Ancient Near Eastern–speak for, "There's so many I can't even count them all!" Countless angels wait upon God: his kingship is that great!

God's infinite greatness is revealed by his eternality. He is described as the "Ancient of Days." The gods of the nations are mere upstarts compared to the God of Israel, who has existed for all of eternity, as Moses prayed, "Lord, you have been our dwelling place throughout all generations. Before the mountains were born or you brought forth the whole world, from everlasting to everlasting you are God" (Ps 90:1–2). Age in the Ancient Near East (like in some cultures still today) was revered and deeply respected. By referring to God as "ancient" and depicting him as an aged (white-haired) man, an implicit comparison is being made: unlike the young pagan gods who deserve no homage because of their youthfulness, the God of Israel is aged—eternal—and worthy of our deepest reverence.

God is eternal. He has always existed and will always exist. It's hard for us to wrap our minds around this truth because human beings, like everything else in the universe, are finite. Everything that has ever existed has a beginning point on the timeline of history—including time itself. God, being eternal, however, has no such starting point. In his essence he stands outside of all historical limitations. And yet, as Christian philosopher William Lane Craig points out, when this eternal, timeless God decided to create, he chose to enter into time to take on a temporal mode of existence in order to relate to us—and more intimately, I might add.[1] How amazing!

God's infinite greatness is revealed by his authority to judge. God's throne is part of a courtroom setting: "The court was seated, and the books were opened" (v. 10c). Although fire often stands for God's perfect moral

---

1. Summarized from an interview of Craig presented in "What Is God's Eternity?"

purity (his holiness), it frequently symbolizes God's fearsome judgment. Thus, John the Baptist and Jesus could speak of the fire of God's judgment (Matt 3:10 and John 15:6, respectively). Similarly, the author of Hebrews, in the context of divine judgment, ominously pronounces, "our 'God is a consuming fire'" (Heb 12:29).

The more power or status people get, the more they tend to see themselves as above the law and exempt from its penalties. When stopped by the police, how many celebrities have condescendingly asked the arresting officer, "Do you know who I am?" fully expecting to skirt around any charges because of their fame or position. Monarchs throughout history have committed atrocities believing that they were the ultimate authority and therefore accountable to no one. Every human being, however, is accountable to the Ancient of Days. According to Daniel's vision, even the nations that wielded power over Israel would be judged by Israel's God.

God has the authority to judge people in this life, and sometimes he may choose to do so. I think we catch a glimpse of this in Luke's Gospel:

> Now there were some present at that time who told Jesus about the Galileans whose blood Pilate had mixed with their sacrifices. Jesus answered, "Do you think that these Galileans were worse sinners than all the other Galileans because they suffered this way? I tell you, no! But unless you repent, you too will all perish. Or those eighteen who died when the tower in Siloam fell on them—do you think they were more guilty than all the others living in Jerusalem? I tell you, no! But unless you repent, you too will all perish." (Luke 13:1–5)

In using these national disasters to call his audience to repentance, Jesus assumes two things: (1) that the Jews who had died in these two tragedies died as a result of their guilt before God; and (2) his listeners were just as guilty as those who had died and, consequently, just as liable to reap similar divine judgment unless they repented.

But God does not always judge people in this life, and this actually seems (albeit anecdotally) to be his preference. The Bible is clear, however, that nothing in this life ever escapes God's judgment in the next, as Hebrews exclaims, "Nothing in all creation is hidden from God's sight. Everything is uncovered and laid bare before the eyes of him to whom we must give account" (Heb 4:13). Whenever God judges he reveals his infinite greatness because he is the final Judge of all humanity.

God Is Infinitely Great

Daniel's vision of God offers us tremendous encouragement for living life in the margins. Bible translator and Anglican clergyman J. B. Phillips wrote a book entitled *Your God Is Too Small*, exposing some of the common false perceptions that even some Christians have about God—beliefs that hinder people from truly experiencing God. One popular misconception is the "God in a box" notion: God has been tamed and trained according to our own liking; he is safe, predictable, and does only what we think he should. Phillips wrote his book in 1952—during Christendom's heyday. If Christians had misunderstandings of God back then, how much more likely are we to have them today, as we try to make sense of our predicament of living in social-cultural exile? The God Daniel saw during the Babylonian exile is anything but small!

While it might seem, because of our present situation, as if God's control over the universe has somehow slipped or loosened, nothing could be further from the truth. God is infinitely great. His eternal reign as king remains as comprehensive now as it ever was. Although he has chosen not to judge our opponents now, that should not be our focus or concern. He will judge everyone in the life to come. Everyone. We must never allow our crisis to determine our theology. Rather, our theology—that God is infinitely great—must determine how we can live wisely in the midst of difficult circumstances.

God's infinite greatness is revealed by the limitless worship he receives. Later in Daniel's vision, one like "a son of man" triumphantly enters the scene. He is led into the presence of the Ancient of Days and is "given authority, glory and sovereign power; all nations and peoples of every language worshiped him" (v. 14a). While there has been considerable debate in academic circles as to the identity of this figure, Jesus' self-identification with this figure during his mock trial (see Matt 26:64 and parallels), leads me to believe that Daniel's "son of man" was the pre-incarnate Christ. The scene finds an echo in the throne room vision in Revelation 4–5, where Jesus (resembling a "lamb looking as if it had been slain") appears in the middle of God's throne, and the angels begin to worship him.

Not only does this son of man figure in Daniel receive worship in the presence of the Ancient of Days, but he is worshiped by all people groups. In other words, although the Jews enjoyed unique covenant privileges with God, this relationship, although special, was not to be considered ethnically exclusive, i.e., as if worship of Yahweh was intended only for Jews and never for Gentiles. For numerous groups of Jews living in exile, the thought of worshiping shoulder to shoulder with their Gentile oppressors would have been shocking, to say the least. Many believed that the only thing awaiting Gentiles in the life-to-come is the wrath of God. Yet Daniel's vision says otherwise. Worshiping the Son of Man is for every nation and every culture. No group is excluded—not even the dreaded Babylonians. In fact, the inclusive nature of salvation has already been observed in the account of the Babylonian King Nebuchadnezzar. Nebuchadnezzar went from being a self-inflated, polytheistic bully to a humble worshiper of the sovereign God of Israel. Worshiping the Son is for everyone.

This universal call for salvation is something we must never forget as we minister from the social and cultural margins of our world. Those who devalue us, who mock us, who seek to squash any remaining influence we might have, are not beyond the grace and grip of God. It's easy for us, because of our exilic quandary, to adopt the mindset the prophet Jonah had towards the Assyrian capital of Nineveh. The Bible paints a grim portrait of Assyria. The prophet Isaiah described the Assyrians as steeped in pride and arrogance, intent on worldwide domination (Isa 10:12–19). Little wonder, then, that the Assyrians destroyed the northern kingdom of Israel, taking thousands of Jews in the Assyrian exile (2 Kgs 17:1–6). Jonah knew how horrible the Assyrians could be—that's why he so stubbornly resisted God's call to preach to Nineveh (Jonah 1:2–3). Jonah wanted God to destroy this evil nation rather than see them repent of their sins and receive his mercy (Jonah 4:1–3, 10–11).

Like Jonah, the temptation for exilic Christians is to hope for a speedy and public vindication: that God himself would silence those who taunt us. The temptation is for us to pray from the margins that God would pour out his stern justice upon those who aggressively oppose us and what we stand for, rather than plead for the Father's mercy on their behalf. But if, as Dutch theologian Abraham Kuyper famously declared, "There is not a square inch in the whole domain of our human existence over which Christ, who is Sovereign over all, does not cry, 'Mine!'" then God's offer of salvation extends even to the church's worst mockers, its worst tormentors, its enemies. Worshiping the Son is for everyone. So then, let our prayers from the margins align with this majestic truth.

When Daniel was given the interpretation of the four beasts, he was told that "the saints of the Most High will receive the kingdom and will possess it forever—yes, forever and ever" (v. 18). Yet before the saints can reign they must first suffer: "As I watched, this horn was waging war against the

God Is Infinitely Great

saints and defeating them, until the Ancient of Days came and pronounced judgment in favor of the saints of the Most High, and the time came when they possessed the kingdom" (vv. 21–22). *God's infinite greatness is revealed through the suffering and celebration of his people.* God has planned a glorious future for his people: they will possess his magisterial kingdom. But this wonderful future is wrapped in defeat: their enemy defeats them in battle. First the saints suffer, then they celebrate. And it is through this divinely appointed order that God's infinite greatness is further revealed.

When believers suffer, this does not mean that they are not in God's will. Unfortunately, large segments of evangelicalism believe otherwise. They preach that suffering is never God's will, and if a Christian suffers, it's because there's either secret sin or a lack of faith. But you would have to rip out an awful lot of pages from the Bible to reach such an incoherent conclusion: entire sections of Scripture are devoted specifically to suffering, like, for example, Job, many of the psalms, the book of Lamentations, large portions of the Prophets, parts of James, 1 Peter, and Revelation.

That suffering gives way to blessing is best seen in the life of Jesus. In the Christ hymn of Philippians 2:6–11, Paul declares that it is precisely because Jesus suffered and died on the cross that God ("therefore") exalted him to the highest place of honor (v. 9a). Likewise, the writer of Hebrews acknowledges that it was "for the joy set before him [that Jesus] endured the cross, scorning its shame, and sat down at the right hand of the throne of God" (Heb 12:2). The author then exhorts believers to consider Jesus as a model for enduring their own suffering (Heb 12:3–4). Thus, even though certain parts of Jesus' ministry are unique and unrepeatable, his suffering as a pattern for us is not. Peter declares that Christ is our model: "To this [suffering] you were called, because Christ suffered for you, leaving you an example, that you should follow in his steps" (1 Pet 2:21). Therefore, like Jesus, first the saints suffer, then they celebrate; and so God's greatness is revealed.

Throne room visions are rare in the Scriptures. Comparing the circumstances of the seers of these visions can prove quite illuminating. The Bible says that when Isaiah saw "the Lord, high and exalted, seated on a throne," it was in the year that King Uzziah died (Isa 6:1). Whenever a beloved political figure dies, the country enters into a period of mourning. For example, 1968 evokes some very painful memories for those involved in the US Civil Rights Movement because that year Martin Luther King Jr. and Robert Kennedy were assassinated. In the wake of those murders, Dick

Holler captured the national sense of loss with his song, "Abraham, Martin, and John," which was recorded by Dion, and reached number four that year on the *Billboard* Hot 100 US singles chart, selling one million copies. Because King Uzziah had been one of Judah's few good kings who sought the Lord and through whom God prospered Israel (2 Chronicles 26), the year he died would have been remembered as a year of immense national mourning.

Stephen the deacon experienced a vision of God's throne room. During a confrontation with his captors, the heavens opened and he "saw the glory of God and Jesus standing at the right hand of God" (Acts 7:55b). Immediately after this sighting he was set upon by the crowd and stoned. In the final book of the Bible, John too saw the throne room of God: "At once I was in the Spirit, and there before me was a throne in heaven with someone sitting on it. And the one who sat there had the appearance of jasper and ruby" (Rev 4:2–3a). When did John receive this glorious revelation of God's throne? The setting for the book of Revelation can be summarized by a single verse: "I, John, your brother and companion in the suffering and kingdom and patient endurance that are ours in Jesus, was on the island of Patmos because of the word of God and the testimony of Jesus" (Rev 1:9). The authorities had been persecuting John and banished him to a lonely existence of exile on the island of Patmos because of his faith in Christ. The setting of Daniel's story, the brutal Babylonian exile, then, corresponds closely with the settings of these other seers.

Each of these glimpses of God's awesome throne took place during a crisis: either in the wake of the death of a beloved figure (for Isaiah), immediately before one's martyrdom (for Stephen), waiting out a lonely existence in exile (for John), or living in the horror of the Babylonian exile. A vision of God's throne was never meant to satisfy a sweet tooth for mystical experiences. It was meant to encourage the discouraged, to uplift the downtrodden, and elevate the depressed. Despite outward circumstances, not only is God in sovereign control of everything, but he has definite plans to exalt his people. Although sometimes it might feel like it, God has neither given up on us nor has he forgotten us. However, first the saints suffer, then they celebrate.

God has sovereignly chosen to reveal his infinite greatness through this divinely appointed order. The height of victory juts out far more against the backdrop of failure. When my wife Lucille and I decided to start having children, we conceived immediately. Nine months later, when we welcomed our first child into the world, I, for the only time in my life, cried tears of joy. As powerful as that event was, I think that for couples who have experienced immense difficulty conceiving—who have tried to get pregnant for many years and have, sadly, miscarried time and again—when they finally give birth for the first time, the joy they feel must be overwhelming, for they know only too well the heartbreak of "failing" again and again. So that first birth means everything to them. They have a much richer appreciation for it, and they celebrate with even more gusto and more vigor than if they had conceived immediately and had given birth right away.

God reveals his infinite greatness not only through this order of suffering before celebration, but he also reveals it through the actual transformation of suffering into glory. I believe the death of Christ remains the very best example of how God, in his infinite greatness, can transform suffering into glory. God accomplished his plan of redemption *precisely* through the death of Jesus. The crucifixion was never "Plan B"—as if "Plan A" was the acceptance of Jesus as Israel's messiah. No, the death of Jesus was "Plan A" right from the beginning—from eternity past—as Peter declares, "[You were redeemed] with the precious blood of Christ, a lamb without blemish or defect. He was chosen before the creation of the world, but was revealed in these last times for your sake" (1 Pet 1:19–20).

Surely the psalmist understates the truth when he proclaims, "Great is the LORD and most worthy of praise; his greatness no one can fathom" (Ps 145:3). The God we serve in our exile is so infinitely great that he can snatch victory from the jaws of defeat. But more than that, God can transform defeat into victory. Could one of the ironies of our exile be not the reestablishment of Christendom after its demise, but the formation of a marginalized church that exhibits and walks in more of Christ's likeness and more of his power than at any time during Christendom?

Questions for Further Reflection

1. According to Daniel's vision, God's throne is mobile. Although God is "mobile," does it seem like he "parks" in some places a lot longer than others? Explain.

2. Have you ever had any misconceptions about God? What were they? Why is it so vital that we have a clear and accurate view of God?

3. How do churches begin to lose sight of God and perceive him incorrectly? What are some ways that churches can regain a clear vision of God?

4. Are there some people you would like to see judged in this life, or some people before whom you would like to stand vindicated now? While God may or may not choose to judge those people in this life, what do you think God wants you to do with these people now? (I.e., how does he want you to behave towards them?)

5. How should knowing that suffering precedes celebration affect how churches go about accomplishing their ministries?

8

God's Timing Is Always Perfect

But I trust in you, LORD; I say, "You are my God." My times are in your hands.

—PS 31:14–15A

"Where is he? Does he know what time it is? He's late!" These thoughts raced through my mind as I anxiously waited for my ride to the airport. I had planned this awesome trip to sunny southern California to visit a school chum. I had never been to California, but, being from the "Great White North" of Canada, I was very excited. My buddy, Jeff, had planned a very detailed itinerary for my visit, trying to pack as much as he could into one week. But now this highly anticipated vacation was circling the drain because my ride was late. "Does he know what time it is?" My ride finally came and off we sped. Doing a fantastic imitation of a Formula One driver, we made amazing time, but, alas, not enough. The damage had been done. I missed my flight.

After I rebooked my flight, I called Jeff and told him of my mishap and that I would be arriving five hours late. He didn't take the news very well. Our itinerary needed revamping according to my new arrival time: the excursion to Venice Beach was now pushed to day two. After I finally arrived, that evening we watched the news over supper and our jaws dropped as we watched the lead story. Gang violence had broken out between the equally notorious Crips and Bloods. The violence resulted in several deaths and

God's Timing Is Always Perfect

many more injuries, and it all took place at . . . Venice Beach—at the very time we had originally planned to be there! We turned to each other and asked, "What if?" What if I hadn't missed my flight and we were at Venice Beach when all of that came down? Would we have been among the numbers who were injured or even killed? What if? I had missed my flight so we thought I was late. But in reality, I was right on time: God's time.

Daniel's second vision takes place two years later and reiterates much of his previous vision of the succession of kingdoms (v. 1a), but the symbolism is different and the focus here is on the final two kingdoms, depicted as a ram and a goat. Most scholars agree that the ram represents the Medo-Persian Empire, while the goat symbolizes the Greek Empire.

That this vision restates the earlier one of chapter 7 implies its significance: God did not want Daniel to miss the message he wanted to share with his people, especially in light of the difficult circumstances in which they found themselves, and would still find themselves. According to the vision, the people of God would endure grave suffering and persecution in the future. During the time of the powerful horn (Antiochus IV Epiphanes), the people of God would be trampled upon by the authorities: "[The horn] grew until it reached the host of the heavens, and it threw some of the starry host down to the earth and trampled on them" (v. 10). Not only would their religious freedoms be curtailed—"[the horn] took away the daily sacrifice" (v. 11b)—but the holy sanctuary would even be desecrated: "and his sanctuary was thrown down" (v. 11b).

We know from history that these sorts of things happened during the reign of Antiochus IV. Prior to Antiochus, the Jews were permitted to live according to Mosaic Law. But this changed with the advent of Antiochus IV, who aggressively instituted diverse and aggressive Hellenistic reforms, whereby the Jews were pressured to adopt a Greek way of life. These reforms climaxed with Antiochus's prohibition against practicing the Jewish religion: he issued an outright ban against burnt offerings, circumcision, and observing the Sabbath. He also had idols built in the Jews' temple. It was definitely a time when "truth was thrown to the ground" (v. 12b).

But what makes this vision stand apart from the earlier one is the specific emphasis on time: "Then I heard a holy one speaking, and another holy one said to him, 'How long will it take for the vision to be fulfilled—the vision concerning the daily sacrifice?' . . . He said to me, 'It will take 2,300 evenings and mornings'" (vv. 13a, 14a). While there is a reference to time in the earlier vision (7:25b), it receives little emphasis. This second vision, however, is actually called by the angel Gabriel, "the vision of the evenings and mornings" (v. 26). In other words, it's noted by its reference to time rather than by its animal or cosmic symbolism, or even by its prediction of the trampling of God's people. The "evening and morning" pairing is not that common in the Bible, appearing most frequently in the creation account, where the pairing appears six times (once for each day of creation). For Daniel's original audience, the phrase "evenings and mornings" would have probably brought to mind thoughts of Genesis 1, and the God of eternity who fashioned both the universe and time itself. Just as he created the dimension of time by which history is measured, so also, *God has appointed the specific timing of every historical event.*

Paul knew this. When he preached to the Athenians on Mars Hill, he noted, "From one man he made all the nations, that they should inhabit the whole earth; and he marked out their appointed times in history and the boundaries of their lands" (Acts 17:26). According to John's Gospel, Jesus was also quite conscious of divinely appointed times. When asked by his mother to perform a miracle, Jesus replied, "My hour has not yet come" (John 2:4b). But later, when some Greeks asked to meet with him, Jesus answered, "The hour has come for the Son of Man to be glorified" (John 12:23b). God had appointed the specific time for Jesus to go to the cross and reveal his glory, and that hour could be neither hastened nor delayed. The time had been firmly fixed by God, the Creator of time. Thus, the Apostle Paul writes, "But when the set time had fully come, God sent his Son, born of a woman, born under the law" (Gal 4:4). Christ came into this world and died on the cross at the exact year, month, day, hour, and second that God had determined. The timing of every historical event belongs to God.

Here in Daniel's second vision of the future, the question is asked, "How long?" (v. 13). "How long?" is probably the most frequently asked question in the Bible, occurring, for example, in Psalms 6:3; 13:1; 35:17; 74:10; 79:5; 80:4; 89:46; 90:13; 94:3; and 119:84; as well as in Habakkuk 1:2 and Revelation 6:10. The question often emerges from difficult conditions: intense emotional, physical, or psychological pain and suffering often brought on (though not always) by persecution of some kind. In Daniel's vision, the conditions are so horrible that the question is raised, not by a sufferer, but by an angelic bystander. How long must these people endure these awful things? We would do well to see beyond the 2,300 evenings and mornings (about six years) that it took for the Jews to capture the temple from the Greeks and restore ritual sacrifice in 164 BC. This interval of time

God's Timing Is Always Perfect

had been sovereignly appointed by God. The length of time for the desecration of the temple and the trampling of the people had been specifically determined to the exact minute by the sovereign God. Because God had appointed the day and time for this interval, the people of God could take courage and face their terrible troubles knowing that these hardships would not go one second longer than the time God had set for them. "My times are in your hands."

Like the geopolitical exiles of the Bible, our own social-cultural exile has always been in God's hands. For the southern kingdom of Judah, the "first wave" of the Babylonian exile came in 608 BC, when Nebuchadnezzar advanced against Jerusalem, sparing King Jehoiakim but carrying off members of Judah's nobility. Less than twenty years later, Nebuchadnezzar landed the most devastating blow of the exile, when he besieged the city, executed large numbers of the leaders, set fire to the holy temple and the royal palace, and took tens of thousands of Jews into captivity, an internment that would last until 538 BC. Did any of these dates catch God by surprise? At any point did God think, "Oh my, I was hoping Nebuchadnezzar wouldn't take Jerusalem as quickly as he did. Man, I really thought the temple would make it at least until the end of the year"? No. All dates and times on the historical timeline have always been subject to divine approval. Their timing belongs to God.

So too, our own exile to the margins was subject to God's consent. The crumbling of Christendom has taken place in waves, over long periods of time, beginning generations ago in Europe. It is still not done. But every pillar that has given way and every fault line that has ruptured has done so right on divine cue. Surely, the Preacher was onto something when he wrote:

> There is a time for everything, and a season for every activity under heaven: a time to be born and a time to die, a time to plant and a time to uproot, a time to kill and a time to heal, a time to tear down and a time to build, a time to weep and a time to laugh.... A time to love and a time to hate, a time for war and a time for peace. (Eccl 3:1–4a, 8)

Sometimes God graciously allows us to see the infinite wisdom of his perfect timing for events that happen. From the time I first felt God's call to teach in the academy to the time I completed my PhD was thirteen years. It then took another five years before I landed my first and current full-time teaching position at Heritage College and Seminary in Cambridge, Ontario.

While I was in the midst of that lengthy journey, periodically I struggled not only with the question "How long, oh Lord?" but even more with "Why so long, Lord?" In my estimation, the process would have been much more streamlined and efficient if God had revealed to me more clearly the nature of my call while still in seminary—then I could have gone straight from there to my doctoral studies in the 1990s. If I had done my PhD at that particular time, only God knows exactly how different my life would have been. But one thing I do know for certain. If I had done my PhD at that time I would never have met my wife Lucille. We met while she was interning at the church in Windsor, Ontario, where I was pastoring. If I had done my doctoral studies in the 90s, then I would never have been in Windsor, so we would never have met: we would never have fallen in love, married, and built the amazing life together we now share with our three wonderful boys. I praise God for his timing because it is perfect! And sometimes he graciously allows us to see this for ourselves.

But there are many other times when God chooses not to reveal to us the wisdom of his timing. Every year approximately half a million people come to New England to watch the famed Boston Marathon. On average, 20,000 runners compete in it each year, making it the third most popular marathon in the US. Some of my friends have raced in the Boston Marathon. Almost 27,000 people participated in 2013, the year of the terrorist bombing. The twin bombs killed three people and seriously injured another 170: competitors, spectators, even children. One family was exiting a restaurant when the bomb exploded only ten feet away. The son suffered shrapnel injuries; the mother broke several bones; the father had his right foot amputated. No doubt for some people it was their first ever Boston Marathon. Of all the years to attend—the wrong place at the wrong time. And probably, for many, there will be no "Aha!" moment when they realize why they had to be there at that time. It is in these sorts of instances when we must choose to trust God.

As the Scriptures teach, God, the Creator of time, appoints our times. His timing is neither spur-of-the-moment nor random. He does not make things up as he goes along in impromptu fashion, spontaneously reacting to the lemons that get thrown his way by making lemonade. Nor is God so busy with all that's involved in running a universe that he can devote little thought to planning the timing of events, and is instead only able to adopt a dartboard approach to determining our times. No. God is infinitely great! Not only does he know everything that will happen, he knows everything

God's Timing Is Always Perfect

that *could* happen (see Matt 11:20–24). The incarnation teaches the holiness and love of God, but it also demonstrates (among other things) God's perfect timing. God appointed Christ to come into our world when: the Romans had established a road system that greatly accelerated travel for its inhabitants; the Roman peace and military presence improved the safety of would-be travelers; and under the Romans Greek continued to be the trade or universal language of the empire, so everybody knew Greek to some extent. These factors (as well as others) enabled the rapid expansion of the church insofar as they enhanced Christian missionary activity. The incarnation was not late, nor was it early. It came, as Paul wrote, in "the fullness of time" (Gal 4:4; ESV) i.e., in God's perfect time.

David sang, "I trust in you, LORD; I say, 'You are my God.' My times are in your hands" (Ps 31:14–15a). We may not always understand God's timing. It may at times seem incomprehensible. Nevertheless, his timing is neither spontaneous nor random. God's timing is always perfect, so we can put our trust in him.

Questions for Further Reflection

1. Was there ever a time in your life when you were waiting for God to do something, and when he finally did he was too late—as least as far as you were concerned? How did you respond to God?

2. Why do you think God often seems to wait so long before he does something?

3. In light of God's omniscience and omnipotence, can he ever really be late about anything? What can you do to become more patient with God's timing in your life?

4. Are there churches or Christian ministries that seem to run ahead of God in terms of following his timing? How can this affect their fruitfulness?

5. How can Christians use this truth, viz., that God's timing is always perfect, to minister from the margins of society more effectively?

9

Pray Wisely

[I]f my people, who are called by my name, will humble themselves and pray and seek my face and turn from their wicked ways, then will I hear from heaven and will forgive their sin and will heal their land.

—2 CHR 7:14

MORE AMERICANS DIED IN the US Civil War than in all of the other wars that the US has participated in, combined: over 600,000 deaths. For the first three years that the war raged, the South was winning decisively, led by their top two generals, Robert E. Lee and Stonewall Jackson. Christian Providential historiographers cite two turning points for the war: The first was President Abraham Lincoln's Emancipation Proclamation of 1862, giving slaves their freedom. The second came on March 30, 1863, when President Lincoln called for a national day of prayer, fasting, and humiliation because of what he perceived to be the sin of slavery and the pride of the nation. Lincoln declared:

> We have been the recipients of the choicest bounties of Heaven; we have been preserved these many years in peace and prosperity; we have grown in numbers, wealth, and power as no other nation has ever grown. But we have forgotten God. We have forgotten the gracious hand which preserved us in peace and multiplied and enriched and strengthened us, and we have vainly imagined, in the deceitfulness of our hearts, that all these blessings were produced

by some superior wisdom and virtue of our own. Intoxicated with unbroken success, we have become too self-sufficient to feel the necessity of redeeming and preserving grace, too proud to pray to the God that made us.

It behooves us, then, to humble ourselves before the offended Power, to confess our national sins, and to pray for clemency and forgiveness.[1]

Two days after this national day of prayer, General Stonewall Jackson died in friendly fire. With the South's outstanding commander out of the picture, the Union army defeated the Confederate forces at Gettysburg, giving the North the crucial victory they needed to turn the course of the Civil War.

Once again we come back to the question of chronology in Daniel: chapter 9 should follow chapter 5, but the author places it here. Why? I think because chapter 9 serves as a segue to the final revelation which encompasses chapters 10–12: chapter 9 ends with the prediction of Cyrus's decree to rebuild the Jerusalem temple, while the setting for Daniel's final revelation (which begins in chapter 10) is the third year of Cyrus.

There are many rich prayers recorded in the Bible, e.g., Ezra 9, Nehemiah 9, and Jesus' prayer in John 17. While all of these and other prayers deserve study in their own right, I think that Daniel's prayer, because of his setting in the Babylonian exile, is of special importance for our times. Daniel's prayer has a number of characteristics that we, as members of a socially and culturally exilic church, ought to take to heart. The first feature of Daniel's prayer concerns its source. First of all, what prompted Daniel to pray?

People pray for different reasons. We pray when we're in need (of a job, a car, money). We pray when we're feeling scared or threatened (by people, by circumstances). Sometimes we pray when we're feeling jubilant and want to give praise to God. There are a variety of reasons why we pray and many of them are quite legitimate. Earlier in the story, we saw why Daniel prayed: in the second chapter he prayed that God would enable him to interpret Nebuchadnezzar's dream so that he and the other court counsellors would not be executed (few prayers are earthier than, "God, I don't want to die!"). And in the sixth chapter we learn that on one occasion Daniel asked God to help him when the king issued a ban against prayer. But here in chapter 9, something else prompted Daniel to pray: "I, Daniel, understood from the Scriptures, according to the word of the Lord given to

---

1. Lincoln, "Proclamation 97."

Pray Wisely

Jeremiah the prophet, that the desolation of Jerusalem would last seventy years. So I turned to the Lord God and pleaded with him in prayer and petition" (vv. 2–3a). What motivated Daniel to pray on this particular occasion was the Scriptures. *Exilic prayer is prompted by Scripture.*

Often our Bible reading remains somewhat disconnected from our prayers. During our devotions, we spend time reading the Bible but then we pray about other, completely unrelated things—many of them legitimate prayer items—and we don't pray about what we just read in the Scriptures. God has given us his inspired Word to teach, rebuke, correct, and train us to live like Christ (2 Tim 3:16–17). Therefore, when we read it, if we don't understand what we've read or if our understanding of the passage seems shallow, we should pray that God would deepen our understanding. If we read of commands to obey or examples to emulate, we should pray that God's Spirit would help us obey these commands or follow in the footsteps of these worthy men and women we have just read about.

Daniel's prayer was prompted by a prophecy of Jeremiah, specifically:

> This is what the LORD says: "When seventy years are completed for Babylon, I will come to you and fulfill my gracious promise to bring you back to this place.... I will gather you from all the nations and places where I have banished you," declares the LORD, "and will bring you back to the place from which I carried you into exile." (Jer 29:10, 14b)

God announced to Jeremiah that the Babylonian exile would last seventy years. When Daniel read this, what did he do? If he were like me, his prayer would have sounded more like, "Yay, God!" After all, if God said it would last for seventy years, then seventy years it would be, period. It's already settled; no need to pray about it, right? Wrong. God's promises did not lead Daniel to satiated inactivity. Rather, God's words served as Daniel's incentive and encouragement to pray about the very thing God had promised.

We are told that God's Word sanctifies us (John 17:17), cleanses us (Eph 5:26), and judges the thoughts and attitudes of our hearts (Heb 4:12). Therefore, when we read the Bible we should pray that it would accomplish these very things in us and in others. We sing about "standing on the promises," and we should. But those divine promises ought to lead us to greater times of prayer, by praying those heavenly promises back to God. Reading the Bible gives us incentive to pray.

The Scriptures not only prompted Daniel to pray but, secondly, they also gave shape to his prayers. *Exilic prayer is shaped by Scripture.* Not only was Daniel familiar with Jeremiah's prophecy, he also knew a little about the book of Kings—especially King Solomon's lengthy prayer for the dedication of the temple. Solomon had prayed, "[LORD, you] keep your covenant of love with your servants who continue wholeheartedly in your way" (1 Kgs 8:23b); Daniel prays, "Lord, the great and awesome God who keeps his covenant of love with all who love him and obey his commands" (v. 4). Solomon had prayed, "We have sinned, we have done wrong, we have acted wickedly" (1 Kgs 8:47b); Daniel prays, "We have sinned and done wrong. We have been wicked" (v. 5a). In fact, in this latter confession, Daniel is actually heeding Solomon's prayer for ending exile:

> When [your people] sin against you ... and if they have a change of heart in the land where they are held captive, and repent and plead with you in the land of their captors and say, "We have sinned, we have done wrong, we have acted wickedly"; and if they turn back to you with all their heart and soul in the land of their enemies who took them captive, and pray to you ... then from heaven, your dwelling place, hear their prayer and their plea, and uphold their cause. And forgive your people, who have sinned against you; forgive all the offences they have committed against you, and cause their captors to show them mercy. (1 Kgs 8:46a, 47–48a, 49–50)

Daniel's prayer, then, is not exactly original. He used the prayers of other Old Testament saints to help him pray. Exilic prayer is shaped by Scripture.

The New Testament contains a number of small but significant prayers (e.g., Eph 1:15–23; 3:14–21; Phil 1:9–11; Col 1:9–12; 2 Thess 2:16–17) that we can use to help shape our prayer life. Paul's prayers are well worth meditating on for the purpose of praying them for ourselves and for others. Take, for example, his prayer for the Philippian church (1:9–11). Against the backdrop of the growing disunity issue in Philippi, Paul essentially prayed that the congregation's love for one another would grow, so that they would be able to discern what is best for Christ's glory and the church's good, in order that they might become more like Jesus while awaiting his Second Coming. The answer to that prayer is a unified church. One of the reasons Paul recorded his prayers was so that churches would join him in praying the way he did. One of our problems (besides not praying enough) is how we pray: many of our prayers are superficial and visionless. To pray like Paul or the rest of the biblical authors means to offer God-centered prayers rooted in the biblical vision and direction for our lives. The Bible is replete with prayers that can help shape our prayer life, imparting that biblical vision and helping us become more like Jesus.

Another feature of Daniel's prayer concerns its attitude, marked by three things. First, *the posture for exilic prayer is one of repentance.* Exile is not pretty. In fact, it is the result of God's people rebelling against him—a rebellion that had escalated with every generation. In the time of the judges, the people of God regularly forsook God in order to run after foreign idols. During the days of Israel's monarchs, these kings (with a few exceptions) got progressively worse morally: from simply permitting the people to worship others gods to encouraging and facilitating national idolatry. Despite repeated warnings from his prophets, rebellion against God compounded. Inevitably, a holy God could no longer refrain from judgment:

> The LORD sent Babylonian, Aramean, Moabite, and Ammonite raiders against [King Jehoiakim]. He sent them to destroy Judah, in accordance with the word of the LORD proclaimed by his servants the prophets. Surely these things happened to Judah according to the LORD'S command, in order to remove them from his presence because of the sins of Manasseh and all he had done. . . . For he had filled Jerusalem with innocent blood and the LORD was not willing to forgive." (2 Kgs 24:2–4)

That God would send his very own people out of the Promised Land and a life of divine blessing into an oppressive existence of exile and a life under a divine curse is nothing short of horrific. Little wonder, then, Daniel prayed with the tone that he did. His prayer lacked the triumphant jubilance that marks so many of the prayers offered in churches today. He adopted a repentant posture before God. He prayed from an utterly broken and contrite heart, from a spirit "covered with shame."

Given the exilic state of affairs, the focus of Daniel's prayer was confession. Five times he spoke of Israel having sinned against God. Twice he stated that his nation had not obeyed God. He described his people as having rebelled against God, as not keeping his laws, as transgressing, as turning away and refusing God, and as having done wrong. He declared, "Our sins and the iniquities of our ancestors have made Jerusalem and your people an object of scorn to all those around us" (v. 16b). Obviously, the gravity of the exile had not been lost on Daniel.

What amazes me about Daniel here is this: as he prayed he adopted his nation's sins and transgressions as his own. More than a dozen times he used "we" or "our" when speaking of Israel's sins and unfaithfulness. From the beginning of the story, we have witnessed Daniel's outstanding piety, humility, compassion, and integrity. Even the angels referred to him as one who is "highly esteemed" (Dan 9:23; 10:10, 19). And yet this servant of God prayed, "[W]e have sinned and done wrong. *We* have been wicked and [*we*] have rebelled; *we* have turned away from your commands and laws. *We* have not listened to your servants the prophets" (vv. 5–6a; emphasis added). As one who stood in the gap as an intercessor, righteous Daniel took ownership of his nation's transgressions: he did not confess "their" sins to God, but rather "our" sins to him. Daniel adopted a repentant posture to pray.

While Daniel does not explicitly ask God to allow the exiles to be released from captivity in order to rebuild Jerusalem and the temple, I think that Daniel actually did pray along these lines. He petitioned God, "For your sake, Lord, look with favor on your desolate sanctuary . . . open your eyes and see the desolation of the city that bears your Name" (v. 17b, 18a), asking that God would "act" and "not delay" (v. 19). When we add these statements to the fact that Jeremiah's prophecy about the exiles' release from seventy years of captivity had prompted Daniel to pray (vv. 2–3a), I think it's fair to say that Daniel probably prayed for the end of the Babylonian captivity.

The basis for Daniel's appeal is God's glory. In other words, *exilic prayer is deeply concerned for God's glory*:

> Now, our God, hear the prayers and petitions of your servant. For your sake, Lord, look with favor on your desolate sanctuary. Give ear, our God, and hear; open your eyes and see the desolation of the city that bears your Name. . . . For your sake, my God, do not delay, because your city and your people bear your Name. (vv. 17, 19b)

At the end of the day, God does what he does for the sake of his own glory. Another term for glory is honor: God seeks his own honor above all things. That God's glory or honor ultimately motivates all of his actions is heard loud and clear throughout the Scriptures. For example, we read in Isaiah:

> For my own name's sake I delay my wrath; for the sake of my praise I hold it back from you, so as not to destroy you completely. See, I have refined you, though not as silver; I have tested you in the furnace of affliction. For my own sake, for my own sake, I do this. How can I let myself be defamed? I will not yield my glory to another. (48:9–11).

While this kind of motivation might make God appear selfish, self-centered, even hypocritical—since he commands us not to seek our own good first but the good of others—we must keep this in mind: if God's glory was not always the laser focus of his heart, then he would actually be guilty of idolatry. We commit idolatry when we make something or someone other than God the ultimate priority in life. For example, if we make money our final goal in life, we are in effect saying, "Money is the most precious, most significant thing in life and therefore, I will orient my life in such a way as to acquire as much money as I possibly can." When a person's life revolves around people or things rather than God, this is idolatry. Well, if God was ultimately driven by his love for us rather than by his own glory, that would mean that his life, his plans, and his purposes would revolve around people rather than himself; and he would be saying, in effect, that people are more important, more significant, and of an intrinsically higher value than he is. But how could that ever be? No, it is not wrong for God to seek his own glory first, above all things; it is absolutely right and just. Exilic prayer, then, must be passionate for God's glory.

Thirdly, *exilic prayer is grounded in God's mercy*. Daniel prayed, "We do not make requests of you because we are righteous, but because of your great mercy. Lord, listen! Lord, forgive!" (vv. 18b–19a). In the Babylonian exile Judah had been decimated by a nation far less righteous than they were. That is why when God revealed to his prophet Habakkuk years earlier that he was planning to discipline his rebellious people with the Babylonians, the prophet was very upset: "Why then do you tolerate the treacherous? Why are you silent while the wicked swallow up those more righteous than themselves?" (Hab 1:13a). The prospect of an even more wicked nation punishing God's people did not seem fair to the prophet; consequently, Habakkuk demanded justice. Daniel saw firsthand the atrocities that the Babylonians committed against the people of God, against the sacred city, and against God's holy temple. He too could have called for justice. But Daniel's prayer was not an indignant demand for justice; it was a humble cry for mercy.

Daniel recognized that God is actually more concerned with the unfaithfulness of his own people than with the immorality of the pagans around them. That makes sense to me. If there was a teenager who was causing all kinds of trouble in my neighbourhood, I would certainly be concerned about him. But if at the same time I was experiencing serious problems with one of my own sons, then my concern for my own son would easily trump the concern I had for that teen who was menacing the neighbourhood. So too, while God is not unconcerned with the injustices propagated by pagans, he is far more concerned with the unfaithfulness of his own people who bear his Name. It is for this reason Peter says that judgment begins with the family of God (1 Pet 4:17a). In the exile Judah had gotten exactly what their rebellion deserved. Now, they didn't need more of God's justice: they needed his mercy, they needed his forgiveness, they needed to be restored. Exilic prayer is grounded in God's mercy.

The final feature of Daniel's prayer concerns its tone. *Exilic prayer should be intense.* We must not think that Daniel simply got down on his knees, prayed these wonderful words, and then got up five minutes later and went about his regular business. Daniel said that he turned to the Lord "in fasting, and in sackcloth and ashes" (v. 3). No one fasts for ten minutes (at least, they're not supposed to): people set out to fast for extended periods of time. Furthermore, when Gabriel came in response to Daniel's prayer, he said, "Daniel, I have now come. . . . As soon as you began to pray, a word went out" (vv. 22b–23a). In verse 22, the use of the term "now," which is emphatic in the Hebrew, implies a lengthy period of time. That is, Gabriel in effect told Daniel, "I have come to you now—not when you first began to pray." Both his fasting and Gabriel's use of "now" suggest a lengthy period of prayer for Daniel.

Fasting is one means by which we humble ourselves before God. By fasting we affirm, like Jesus did in the wilderness, that no one lives on "bread alone but on every word that comes from the mouth of God" (Matt 4:4b). We give up a necessity like food (or extras like TV, chocolate, or the Internet) in order to give ourselves more fully to God in prayer, thereby acknowledging our supreme need for him in our lives. Wearing sackcloth and covering oneself in ashes was an expression of intense mourning. For example, when Job's three friends heard of his misery and went to comfort him, "they began to weep aloud, and they tore their robes and sprinkled dust on their heads" (Job 2:12b). Later, after God sternly rebuked Job for speaking in ignorance, Job confessed his sin and repented "in dust and ashes" (Job 42:6b). Dust and ashes physically symbolize internal anguish. Thus, Daniel 9 represents only a snippet of what would have been for Daniel a very prolonged and intense time of prayer.

The sins of our society have escalated in terms of frequency and shamelessness. While I'm sure child abductions have been with us for generations, nowadays it seems like it happens more often and more brazenly. Not too long ago, I recall a Toronto news radio station reporting two separate instances of attempted child abductions that occurred in broad daylight, in public view—and within arm's reach of the child's parent/grandparent. And although it's imperative that we pray against social evils, it's even more important that we, as exiles, seek God with a repentant heart for the spiritual restoration of his people. Could it be that we need to recognize, as Daniel before us, that God's people, more than ever before, needs an overflowing portion of his mercy?

The Western church finds itself in social-cultural exile because of its failure to live like Christ before a watching world. What we now need are churches ready to engage in the kind of penitential prayer that Daniel did. We need churches that recognize our grievous sins: how the church of the West, steeped in its arrogance, has failed God for generations. We need churches that will set their face to walk resolutely in humble repentance before God, to own the sins of their forefathers in the faith, the way Daniel did. We need churches that will not pray, "God, forgive *them* for *their* pride and *their* unfaithfulness," but rather, "God, forgive *us* for *our* pride and *our* unfaithfulness." In reality, we need less of God's justice to be poured out on society and more of God's mercy to be poured out on his unfaithful church. We need more of God's mercy to help us become what we failed to become in generations past: a people who corporately reflect the life, light, and love of their Lord Jesus Christ to the world.

The prayer of Daniel instructs us how to pray as we live in the margins. But more than that, when we add a few other pieces to the puzzle, his prayer offers us hope. Ultimately, Daniel's prayer was answered. In fact, we can deduce a timeframe for the answer: Daniel prayed for restoration in the first year of Darius (9:1), and Darius reigned for two years before giving way to Cyrus, who issued the edict in the first year of his reign to permit the Jews to return to Jerusalem to rebuild the temple (see Ezra 1:1–4). That means that Daniel waited two years for God to answer his prayer. That's actually not too shabby. Many of us have had to pray for much longer than that to see some of our prayers answered. So in the physical realm, God's response time to Daniel's prayer was measured in years.

In the heavenly realm, however, the response time was much quicker. It was during Daniel's intense time of prayer and fasting that God sent him the angel. While Gabriel stated that an answer was given as soon as Daniel began to pray (v. 23a), he did not come to him until some time later (the "now" in v. 22). While we don't know exactly how long it took Gabriel to reach Daniel, we can be sure that the time frame here is in days, not years. Things seem to move faster in the heavenly realm than in the physical realm, and because of that we can be encouraged to "walk by faith and not by sight" in the margins.

Of note as well is the answer that Gabriel offered Daniel. It is not exactly what Daniel sought: the angel offered him a word of "insight and understanding" (v. 22). Getting into the specifics of Gabriel's prophetic word would take us too far a field for our purposes here. Suffice it to say, his essential message to Daniel was this: the Babylonian exile will indeed end at the appointed time, and the Jerusalem temple and the sacrificial system will be restored; but more times of distress await God's people, culminating in the cessation of sacrifice and the awful desecration of the new (second) temple, followed eventually by an outpouring of God's judgment upon the perpetrators.

Thus, Gabriel's word of "insight and understanding" to Daniel, in response to his penitential prayers, could perhaps be summed up like this: "Daniel, the exile will end at its foreordained time and my people will again be restored. But don't think that restoration means no more problems. More problems are on the way, but I shall tend to these as well in due course." In other words, the exile came by God's design and would end by God's design. The end of the exile and the restoration of God's people would be a miraculous blessing, but it would not spell the end of evil and suffering—not in this life anyway.

While God eventually answered Daniel's prayer about the end of the Babylonian exile and the restoration of his people, I cannot stress enough the sovereignty of God. It's not that Daniel's wise prayers hastened God's hand, as if forcibly moving the divine clock ahead one hour ahead of schedule. It did not. The end of the exile came at the appointed time, as first predicted by Jeremiah (29:10–14). Doubtless many other pious believers (like Jeremiah) had prayed for the end of the exile but never lived to see it. Daniel had the advantage of being born late enough in history to see his prayers answered. Had he been born much earlier, he would never have seen his prayers answered. Similarly, we can and should pray for the end our own exile and for the restoration of God's people, but we must not presume that we will see the answer to these prayers. The answer may very well be for a future generation. Regardless, God still calls out to his exilic church, "If my people, who are called by my name, will humble themselves and pray and seek my face and turn from their wicked ways, then will I hear from heaven and will forgive their sin and will heal their land" (2 Chr 7:14).

Questions for Further Reflection

1. List some of the things that prompt you to pray. Where does Scripture fall in your list? What are some ways that you can benefit from praying Scripture?

2. When praying on behalf of your church or your country, have you ever taken ownership of their sins? In other words, do you pray, "Forgive *them their* sins," or do you pray, "Forgive *us our* sins"? Why is it important to own their sins?

3. How would you describe the intensity or passion with which you pray? Is it polite chitchat, meaningful conversation, Gethsemane-like intercession, or something else? What are some steps you can take to increase the intensity of your prayers?

4. Should churches engage in penitential prayer like Daniel? How?

5. Does praying like Daniel help to facilitate a wise witness to society? Why or why not?

10

Pray Alertly

For our struggle is not against flesh and blood, but against the rulers, against the authorities, against the powers of this dark world and against the spiritual forces of evil in the heavenly realms.

—EPH 6:12

THINGS WERE NOT GOING as planned. My short-term missions team had prepared diligently for our trip to France, where we would be leading a summer camp for fifty youth. We had been very excited to go and expected God to do some great things. Unfortunately, despite all of our preparation and prayer, we didn't sense that we had been getting anywhere with the youth at the camp. Our worship times seemed wooden; the speaker was not connecting with the teens; and the small groups were behaving more like play groups. To top it off, team members began bickering with each other, and the unity we once had was quickly dissipating. The turning point for the mission came when we recognized that the powers of darkness had dug in and were fighting back furiously. When we began to pray specifically against the evil spirits that were wrestling against us (and told our intercessors back home in Ottawa to do the same), the spiritual tide turned and we began to see God move powerfully on the youth, and the lives of young people were deeply touched. It wasn't until we directed our energy to battling against the strategies of our unseen enemy, rather than against each other, that people came to Christ.

We've Lost. What Now?

The sequence of events outlined at the outset of chapter 10 is significant. The narrative opens with a statement that a revelation was given to Daniel (v. 1a), but that the interpretation of that revelation came to Daniel later by way of a vision (v. 1b). The story then outlines how Daniel received that interpretation: "At that time I, Daniel, mourned for three weeks. I ate no choice food; no meat or wine touched my lips; and I used no lotions at all until the three weeks were over" (vv. 2–3). Daniel did not instantly understand God's message to him (i.e., the initial revelation) so he sought God for its meaning. This is similar to what we observed earlier: God sometimes speaks in the symbol-laden language of dreams and visions in order to humble us and to engage our minds. Moreover, what was implicit in the previous chapter now becomes explicit here: Daniel sought God for an extended period of time before God finally answered his prayers. According to the text, it took three weeks of intense prayer, mourning, and fasting to receive a response from God. I think the principle here is this: *God uses delays to teach us important life lessons.*

In our technologically driven world, we have become used to getting everything "now": from microwave meals to fast food restaurants to high-speed Internet. But things don't always work like that in the spiritual realm. Sometimes they do. My very first answer to prayer took all of about ten seconds to receive. I became a Christian on the final day of a vacation Bible school in my hometown of Windsor, Ontario. That afternoon, on my way home, while waiting for a traffic light to turn green so I could cross a busy street, I noticed an orange in the middle of the road. Many cars were zipping by on both sides, always missing it. Like the twelve-year-old boy that I was, I silently prayed, "Lord, I know you're in my heart now, but, could you prove it by making the next car hit that orange?" The very next car: splat!

Sometimes things in the spiritual realm move quickly, but at other times they do not, especially when dealing with matters of life more complex than an orange. It's not because God finds these issues more difficult to handle; after all, there are no degrees of difficulty for an omnipotent being. Rather, it's because in these larger matters God wants to teach us vital lessons; and effective learning usually presupposes time (see, for example, the elementary, secondary, and post-secondary school systems). Often it takes us lengthy periods of time to learn something well, to internalize it. Moses knew God had called him to lead his people out of Egypt, but he had to work another forty years in the wilderness as a shepherd before he actually did so. Despite being anointed by the prophet Samuel as Israel's new king,

David didn't actually ascend to the throne for another decade, spending those years on the run for his life from King Saul. God uses delays to teach us important life lessons.

One important lesson God often teaches us through delays has to do with trust. *Delays reveal the true object of our trust.* The issue many of us face is whether to trust God or trust in self. I've known many Christians who have endured long bouts of unemployment. While God is probably teaching different believers different things during these difficult times of joblessness, doubtless for many Christians the core issue is trust. For these brothers and sisters, if God provided a job immediately then they might consciously or subconsciously assume that they earned that job through their own know-how, their own skills, their own experience, their own ability to shine under pressure in an interview. In other words, they won that job by relying on themselves. But what about God? Shouldn't we ultimately be relying on—trusting in—God? Delays remind us that it's "[n]ot by might nor by power, but by [God's] Spirit" (Zech 4:6b). Ultimately, our trust must rest in God.

For our purposes here, the main lesson to learn from the text has to do with the reason for the three-week delay in the answer to Daniel's prayers. Again, what was implicit in the previous chapter (9:23) becomes explicit here:

> Since the first day that you set your mind to gain understanding and to humble yourself before your God, your words were heard, and I have come in response to them. But the prince of the Persian kingdom resisted me twenty-one days. Then Michael, one of the chief princes, came to help me, because I was detained there with the king of Persia. (vv. 12–13)

Spiritual warfare causes delays. God had heard Daniel's prayers immediately, but an angelic struggle in the heavenly realm ensued, causing a delay. As soon as Daniel began to pray, God dispatched an angel in response to his prayer; however, a funny thing happened on the way to Daniel: the angel had a run-in with the "prince/king of Persia." Who is this mysterious figure who had the power to stop an angel in its tracks?

I believe this individual was a demon (i.e., a fallen angel), for three reasons. First, it can't be speaking literally because the king of Persia at that time was already identified as Cyrus, whom Daniel faithfully served and who ended the Babylonian exile, allowing the Jews to return to Palestine. Second, given the immense power that angels possess (e.g., 2 Kgs

19:35 records how a single angel destroyed 185,000 soldiers in one night), it doesn't seem possible that a human king could have put up that much resistance against one of God's heavenly warriors. And third, the Apostle Paul spoke of heavenly, invisible thrones, rulers, and authorities that seem to parallel earthly ones (see Col 1:16). That is why I think that God's angel, while on its way to Daniel, got into a cosmic tussle with a demon. Thus, in chapter 10 we get a very helpful glimpse into some of the activities and goings-on in the spiritual realm. Some delays in the answers to our prayers are the direct result of demonic activity, i.e., spiritual warfare.

Not that all delays are caused by demonic activity. Jesus on a number of occasions taught about persistence in prayer; for example, in the parable of the persistent widow (Luke 18:1–8). Like the widow who eventually wore down the unjust judge through her incessant cries for justice, this parable teaches us that Christians are supposed to prevail in prayer. Why? One reason, according to this parable, is the connection between persistence in prayer and persevering faith. In other words, faith in Christ must persevere to the end, but faith cannot persevere without persistent prayer: the two are closely intertwined. If God always answered our prayers immediately then we would never learn to persevere in prayer, and ultimately, to persevere in our faith.

Nevertheless, as we strive to follow God's leading, we will experience resistance in the heavenly realm, the ramifications of which inevitably spill over into the earthly realm, resulting in, for example, delays in seeing our prayers answered—similar to what Daniel experienced. Thus, *spiritual warfare can create earthly problems.* The Apostle Paul encountered fierce spiritual warfare during his missionary journeys. When addressing the church in Thessalonica, he candidly wrote, "[O]ut of our intense longing we made every effort to see you. For we wanted to come to you—certainly I, Paul, did, again and again—but Satan blocked our way" (1 Thess 2:17b–18). I find these verses a bit disturbing. Paul desperately wanted to see his spiritual children and made efforts to do so, but on every front Satan stopped him from visiting the church. We're not told how Satan accomplished this feat, only that he did so several times.

Spiritual warfare can create problems like earthly opposition. If Satan and his minions achieved this level of success against the likes of Paul during apostolic times, then what kind of successes might he have—indeed, might he have already accomplished—during our own days of exile? The fact that the Western church dwells in the margins of our society testifies, at least to some degree, to the measure of success Satan has had against the church. Therefore, we should expect a high level of demonic resistance as we go about kingdom business. Some conflict will be this-worldly. Sometimes congregations, for example, when they outgrow their original lot and seek to expand, encounter fierce opposition from the local neighbours. This type of earthly hostility, I believe, is a manifestation of war in the heavenlies.

Besides earthly opposition, according to the text, demonic resistance can manifest physically. During Daniel's three-week period of seeking God for the meaning of the revelation, he showed signs of physical and emotional exhaustion: "I had no strength left, my face turned deathly pale and I was helpless. . . . How can I, your servant, talk with you, my lord? My strength is gone and I can hardly breathe" (vv. 8b, 17). This closely echoes Daniel's earlier experience with the vision of the ram and goat: "I, Daniel, was worn out. I lay exhausted for several days" (8:27a). Not only was Daniel's answer delayed by three weeks, but because of intense spiritual warfare, the earthly fallout included physical and emotional exhaustion. This shouldn't be entirely surprising since humans are, to put it glibly, spirits wrapped in bodies. Our spirit and our body are closely intertwined, as the Scriptures affirm, "[F]ear the Lord and shun evil. This will bring health to your body and nourishment to your bones" (Prov 3:7b–8). In other words, fearing God and living morally—both spiritual activities—results in physical health.

Because of the intimate relationship between spirit and body, many times what afflicts the body distresses the spirit, and what distresses the spirit affects the body. As a former pastor, I can attest that there have been times when believers have suffered physically—headaches, nausea, etc.—just as they were about to engage in significant ministry of some kind. But as soon as we began to engage in spiritual warfare, targeting our prayers specifically against the evil forces that had come against us because of our ministry, physical relief came.

Because of the sometimes heightened level of spiritual warfare in the margins, believers must take seriously Paul's caution to the church in Ephesus: "For our struggle is not against flesh and blood, but against the rulers, against the authorities, against the powers of this dark world and against the spiritual forces of evil in the heavenly realms" (Eph 6:12). For the exilic church to thrive, we must understand that the battle must be fought first and foremost in the spiritual arena, not the political one. Christians and churches who choose to wage the political battle without first and continually taking up arms in the spiritual realm will, at best, not be as effective as they could be, and at worst, bring reproach to the cause of Christ. That is why the Apostle ends his discussion of spiritual warfare with the admonition: "And pray in the Spirit on all occasions with all kinds of prayers and requests. With this in mind, be alert and always keep on praying for all the Lord's people" (Eph 6:18). In other words, for warfare to be waged effectively the prayer warrior must: pray frequently, pray according to the Spirit's promptings, pray specifically, pray alertly, and pray for other believers in need of the prayers of someone who knows how to engage in spiritual warfare on their behalf.

While it may disturb some people to speak of demonic forces defeating the people of God, we must always view this in the context of God's absolute sovereignty. To this end, Paul's life offers us further insight. Paul told the Corinthians that a thorn in his flesh, which he identified as a "messenger of Satan," was sent to torment him (2 Cor 12:7). Three times he prayed for it to be taken away, and each time God's answer was "No." The reason: "My grace is sufficient for you, for my power is made perfect in weakness" (2 Cor 12:9a). Don't miss what's going on here: Paul was experiencing some sort of painful, demonic oppression, causing him to pray repeatedly for relief from it; but he failed to experience any. In other words, he lost the battle with a demonic foe (yet again: remember 1 Thess 2:17–18?). In the context of God's absolute sovereignty, however, God permitted Paul's defeat because through it he was actually perfecting Paul. Through these "defeats" God was making Paul less like Paul and more like Jesus, as the Apostle himself testifies: "Therefore I will boast all the more gladly about my weaknesses, so that Christ's power may rest on me. . . . For when I am weak [in myself], then I am strong [in Christ]" (2 Cor 12:9b, 10b). God perfects us even through our defeats.

Because Daniel's people had rebelled against God for generations, violating their holy covenant and living as faithless idolaters, God gave them over to the exile (2 Kgs 24:1–4). The Babylonian exile represented God's holy judgment against them. Similarly, I believe that because the Western church has rebelled against God for generations through its exceeding hubris, unbelief, and immorality, God, in his holy judgment, has given us over into the hands of secular society, exiling us to its social and cultural margins. Yet, there is another dynamic simultaneously at work: our egregious sins have permitted Satan and his minions more than just a foothold (Eph 4:27)—the enemy has been allowed to come in like a flood and have at us, thus intensifying and perpetuating our exile. Satan believes he's winning, that he's defeating us. But could it be that God is sovereignly using our exilic "defeat" at the hand of our spiritual adversary to perfect us and to make us more like his son Jesus? "For when I am weak, then I am strong."

Ultimately, our battle from the margins is not against our earthly opponents—our "captors"—but against the evil spirits of darkness in the heavenly realms. To that end we must heed the words of the Apostle Paul, that old veteran of spiritual warfare: "And pray in the Spirit on all occasions with all kinds of prayers and requests . . . be alert and always keep on praying for all the Lord's people" (Eph 6:18).

Questions for Further Reflection

1. Why are some of our prayers answered quickly while others take a long time to answer? What are some of the lessons to learn while waiting for God to answer prayer?

2. Was there ever a time that you witnessed or experienced some form of spiritual resistance or warfare? Describe the incident. What was your response? Are there ways that you could improve your response or increase your effectiveness in spiritual warfare?

3. When we seem to be losing the battle, is God still in control? If so, why does he permit us to suffer loss?

4. What are some evidences of the earthly fallout of heavenly warfare in some churches? Are there signs of warfare in your own church? What are some steps you and/or your church can take to improve the situation?

5. Where do you discern the spiritual battles in our culture to be? How can local congregations engage in these battles more effectively?

11

There's Hope for the Persecuted

"For I know the plans I have for you," declares the LORD, "plans to prosper you and not to harm you, plans to give you hope and a future."

—JER 29:11

THE AWFUL IMAGES OF 9/11 are forever etched in our minds. When it happened, I remember how the front page of nearly every newspaper featured pictures of people leaping from the blazing World Trade Center towers, plummeting to their death. One survivor of the tragedy, Andrew, shared his experience during an interview. Andrew had taken it upon himself to try to talk people down from jumping. In some instances he was successful. In others he was not. The interviewer asked him, "Why on earth would people jump a hundred stories to their death?" With a subdued seriousness, Andrew replied, "Because they had no hope."[1]

Daniel was given a revelation that he did not understand (10:1a). Consequently, he sought God for its meaning through prayer and fasting until, in response to his prayers, an angel came to him in a vision with the interpretation of the revelation (10:1b–3). All of chapter 11 through the first third of chapter 12 represents the angel's interpretation of Daniel's revelation.

When you read the angel's interpretation, you cannot help but be struck by the amazing breadth of God's sovereignty over human affairs.

1. Based on the author's recall of an episode of the *The Oprah Winfrey Show*.

The description of the history entailed in his message is punctuated with the language of predestination: "in fulfillment of the vision" (11:14); "an end will still come at the appointed time" (11:27); "at the appointed time" (11:29); "[the end] will still come at the appointed time" (11:35); "roll up and seal the words of the scroll until the time of the end" (12:4). One of the truths that ring loud and clear in the Bible is the sovereignty of God. God's specific control over the totality of his creation is either explicitly taught or presupposed on nearly every page of Scripture. So specific is God's control over his creation that Jesus said even a lowly sparrow does not fall to the ground apart from the will of our heavenly Father (Matt 10:29).

God's sovereignty is one of the major themes of the book of Daniel. Earlier in the story Daniel praised God because "He changes times and seasons; he deposes kings and raises up others" (2:21a). When Nebuchadnezzar's sanity was restored, he praised God because he came to realize that "he does as he pleases with the powers of heaven and the peoples of the earth" (4:35). The fact that God does as he pleases with the nations of the earth comes to the fore in this final vision of Daniel's prophecy. The language of predestination in the vision means that the events of the future are not merely foreseen by God like some cosmic fortune-teller; rather, they have been specifically planned by him and therefore come about (as predicted by the angel) in fulfilment of his sovereign purposes. *God's sweeping control over all earthly affairs offers us hope in exile.*

In Daniel's prophecy, God's sovereignty manifests in three ways. First, *God oversees the successions of power within the nations.* The vision outlines the successions of power that took place in the nations that ruled Israel. At the time of Daniel's vision, Israel was subject to the Persians under the auspices of Cyrus. Cyrus's rule would be followed by four more kings of Persia, the last of which was Xerxes (485–464 BC). The "mighty king" who would succeed Xerxes was none other than Alexander the Great, who is described in the same terms that Nebuchadnezzar had used for God in 4:35: he will "do as he pleases" (v. 3). After Alexander's demise in 323 BC, his empire was divided between his four generals (Antipater, Lysimachus, Seleucus Nicator, and Ptolemy), who did not exercise the same immense power or authority that Alexander had wielded (v. 4).

This type of divinely managed succession of power has already been evidenced in the story. In chapter 2, God showed Nebuchadnezzar through a dream the succession of powers that would follow him. In chapter 5, God informed King Belshazzar that the Babylonian kingdom was about to be

There's Hope for the Persecuted

taken over by the Medes. In chapter 8, Daniel saw in a vision how the empire of the Medes would give way to the Persian Empire, which itself would be conquered by Alexander the Great, whose kingdom ultimately ended up in the hands of the murderous Antiochus Epiphanes. God's sovereign administration extends far beyond the activities of his own people to even the other nations of the world. That is why the Apostle Paul could write, regarding governmental affairs, "[T]here is no authority except that which God has established. The authorities that exist have been established by God" (Rom 13:1b). Ironically, Paul wrote these words during the reign of Emperor Nero, who ferociously persecuted Christians and ultimately ordered Paul's own execution. Thus, kings and queens, presidents and prime ministers, chancellors and chiefs—past, present, and future—come to power, ultimately, because God has specifically (albeit sometimes incomprehensibly) placed them in these positions.

Not only does God administer successions of power in a general way, but second, the predestinarian language that punctuates the vision implies that *God directs the specific means used to gain political power*. In other words, even political strategies are subject to God's sovereign hand. This can be seen in 11:5–20, which describes the wars between the Ptolemies and the Seleucids. The period of the struggles between these two dynasties was quite chaotic: five wars encompassing twenty years fought over a span of about seventy-five years (274–200 BC).

The vision mentions several means used to achieve political power. One way was through marriage (vv. 5–6). In 252 BC, Ptolemy II struck a peace treaty with Antiochus II, with the terms that Antiochus was to marry Ptolemy's daughter, Berenice. But there was one problem: Antiochus was already married to Laodice. Laodice didn't take too kindly to being divorced, so she secretly conspired against Berenice and her infant son (fathered by Ptolemy) and had them assassinated. It was in this way that Berenice was "betrayed" (v. 6) and this political alliance was short-lived.

Political rule was and still is most often attained through military might (vv. 7–20). After the death of Ptolemy II, his son Ptolemy III avenged the death of his sister, Berenice, and successfully waged war against the Seleucids from 246 to 241 BC. In the generation that followed, Ptolemy IV soundly defeated the forces of Antiochus III (vv. 11–12). But the Seleucids, under Antiochus III, eventually gained the upper hand: "The forces of [Ptolemy V] will be powerless to resist; even their best troops will not have the strength to stand" (v. 15b). Antiochus III, who established himself over

Palestine ("the Beautiful Land" [v. 16]), is described with the expression used for Alexander the Great (in v. 3): "[he] will do as he pleases" (v. 16a). But eventually, "a commander will put an end to his insolence and will turn his insolence back on him" (v. 18b): in 189 BC his army of 70,000 suffered great losses at the hands of a Roman contingent only half its size. Antiochus III eventually met an ignominious end, when, unable to make indemnity payments to Rome, he attempted to plunder the temple of Bel in Elymais, but the local inhabitants defended their temple, killing Antiochus in the process. Hence, the prophecy for Antiochus was fulfilled: "[he] will stumble and fall, to be seen no more" (v. 19).

Thus, God does much more than just passively watch over the processes of royal successions: he mysteriously stands behind their very means. God does not rule over the nations in some distant and disinterested way; he rules over them in a close, active, and specific way. There are many more explicit instances in Scripture that illustrate God's specific sovereignty over these sorts of affairs. For example, in the time of the judges of Israel we are told that a young Philistine woman caught Samson's eye such that he desired to have her for a wife. His parents objected to his intentions since the Law of Moses forbade intermarriage with Gentiles. But Samson insisted on taking this Gentile woman as a wife. Although Samson clearly violated Mosaic Law, the narrator informs the reader that "this was from the LORD, who was seeking an occasion to confront the Philistines" (Judg 14:4). In other words, God mysteriously stood behind Samson's unlawful choice in order to bring about Israel's deliverance from the Philistines through Samson.

Similarly, near the end of this same period, in preparing the way for Samuel's rule as Israel's leader, the author of 1 Samuel writes that Eli's two sons, who were Samuel's priestly predecessors, did not listen to their father's rebuke of their flagrantly immoral actions "for it was the LORD'S will to put them to death" (1 Sam 2:25b). Thus, it was not the Lord's will for Eli's sons to heed their father's rebuke and repent of their sin; rather, it was God's will for the two priests to ignore Eli and die for their sins, thus paving the way for Samuel's succession as Israel's priest and judge. Knowing that our loving, heavenly Father wields such awesome yet intimate control over earthly affairs offers us a tremendous sense of hope in dire times.

When Bill Clinton defeated incumbent George H. W. Bush in the 1992 US presidential election, one evangelical commentator remarked that "God's will was not done." It was not God's will for Clinton to win the

There's Hope for the Persecuted

election but Bush. God's will was not done? Hmm, let's explore that for a minute. If God's will was for the re-election of George Bush, but Bill Clinton won, that would mean that God's plan had been thwarted, and that he, in effect, "lost one." Well, if God lost one in 1992, what about 1991, or 1990, or 1890, or 1790? Is it possible that God might have lost at other times in history? Moreover, if God's purposes were defeated on the grand, national stage of a country like the US, then what about the outworking of his plans on the much smaller battlefields and back alleys of the lives of individual people? In other words, how many times has God been thwarted in your life or in mine? Can God, then, really promise or guarantee anything at all? What a frightening scenario. Thankfully, we never have to go there, because, as the story of Daniel teaches, God mysteriously yet nonetheless specifically directs the successions of power that take place within nations.

A third manifestation of God's sovereignty in this passage is this: during a period of tremendous political upheaval in which the people of God fell victim to their oppressors, *God permitted the persecution of his people.* The terrifying reign of Antiochus IV is described in 11:21–35. What kind of man was Antiochus IV? Well, for starters, history tells us that he put his image on the coins he had minted, along with inscription *Theos Epiphanes*— Greek for "God Manifest." So, obviously he thought he was all that—and a god besides. Here in this vision we are given a peek at the kind of monarch he was. He was ruler who gained victories through deception (v. 21), who used trickery to get ahead (v. 23), and who lied to gain the upper hand (v. 27) (Hmm, I guess politics really hasn't changed that much). But the kicker was his intense hatred for the people of God and their religion: "his heart will be set against the holy covenant . . . and [he will] vent his fury against [them]" (vv. 28, 30).

How did Antiochus vent his fury against God's people? Initially, as he started to turn up the heat against the Jews, he rewarded those Jews who forsook their religion (v. 30b). Later his army desecrated God's temple, abolishing the daily sacrifice and setting up the "abomination that causes desolation" (v. 31). History confirms that in 168 BC Antiochus IV marched against Jerusalem and slaughtered 80,000 Jews and robbed the temple of its golden vessels and other sacred objects. Further, he built a statue of Zeus inside the temple—the "abomination that causes desolation"—thereby ensuring the cessation of the Jews' daily ritual sacrifice to God. He also changed the name of the Jerusalem temple to the Temple of Zeus Olympus. The angel thus summarizes Antiochus's destructive rampage: "[The people of God] will fall by the sword or be burned or captured or plundered" (v. 33b).

We've Lost. What Now?

And yet, despite the horrific persecution experienced by God's people, none of it had been beyond the purview of God's watchful eye. None of it bypassed his sovereign hand. Antiochus's invasions came "at the appointed time" (v. 29). The Jews who fell away during the reign of Antiochus III and rebelled against God did so only "in fulfillment of the [angel's] vision" (v. 14). The persecution of the people of God "will be successful until the time of wrath is completed, for what has been determined must take place" (v. 36b). These are powerful words that need to be taken to heart. The persecution of God's people will be successful only until God's appointed time of wrath has been concluded. While persecution of any kind is never pleasant, sufferers can be assured that what is happening is indeed part of God's plan for them—a plan that can, at times, seem inexplicable.

Our suffering does not mean that God has stopped caring about us or that the wells of his love have finally run dry. It does not mean that the enemy has managed to slip one under God's goalie pad because God is being peppered with so many shots from every direction simultaneously. It does not mean that Satan has somehow pinned God against the ropes and is now taking the fight to God. Suffering is part of God's sovereign plan. As I mentioned earlier in chapter 7, entire books of the Bible are largely predicated on this truth. God has ordained suffering. This is a mysterious truth, far too complex to be solved by mortal minds. But Scripture is replete with accounts of God not simply using suffering but ordaining it. For the sake of space, I'll offer only two examples.

At the end of the book of Genesis, Joseph looked back at the suffering he experienced at the hands of his jealous brothers—being thrown into a pit and sold into slavery—and he assured them, "You intended to harm me, but God intended it for good" (Gen 50:20a). I have often heard this verse quoted as, "You intended to harm me but God *used* it for good," implying that the harm Joseph suffered was not God's will for him but God managed to use it anyway. But that's not what the text says! The original Hebrew uses the word translated "intend" (meaning "think," "reckon," "account") twice: once for Joseph's brothers ("you *intended* to harm me") and once for God ("God *intended* it for good"). In other words, in that one act of evil there were two intentions: the brothers' and God's. The brothers' intentions were evil, thereby producing the evil act, while God's intentions within that same act resulted in good: the salvation of Jacob and his family.

This phenomenon of human and divine intentions in a single act is most plainly seen in the second example: the crucifixion of Christ. In the

There's Hope for the Persecuted

book of Acts, the disciples confessed in their prayer, "Indeed Herod and Pontius Pilate met together with the Gentiles and the people of Israel in this city to conspire against your holy servant Jesus, whom you anointed. They did what your power and will had decided beforehand should happen" (4:27–28). The religious leaders conspired to do evil to Jesus, but their evil conspiracy was in full accord with God's sovereign purposes, for it was precisely through their evil that God intended to bring about salvation. In one act (the crucifixion) there were two completely antithetical intentions: one evil (the religious leaders'), and one good (God's). Thus, God ordains suffering.

Doubtless, some measure of Christ's suffering was historically unique because of his identity as God Incarnate and his mission to accomplish salvation. Nevertheless, his suffering remains a model for his followers and is integral to our calling as Christians: "[I]f you suffer for doing good and you endure it, this is commendable before God. To this you were called, because Christ suffered for you, leaving you an example that you should follow in his steps" (1 Pet 2:20b–21). Thus, as it was with Jesus, so it is with us: God is mysteriously at work in and through our suffering, for his sovereign hand extends even to our darkest moments. That is precisely why there is hope for the persecuted.

Persecution takes many forms. For some, especially young people, it can come in the form of icy stares, cruel taunts, or isolation—which makes it difficult for many Christian teenagers to stand up openly for Christ in their schools. When I was a youth pastor, one of the things I used to do was have lunch with my students in their school. The administration at one high school, however, thought my mere presence in the school cafeteria would make other students uncomfortable, so they segregated us to a separate room. For others, persecution is expressed in unjust workplace practices. I know Christians who, because of openly identifying with Christ in the workplace, and because of holding to a higher moral ground than many of their coworkers, consistently end up getting the worst job assignments, to be completed under inordinately difficult conditions. Recently the US Court of Appeals for the Fourth Circuit overturned a lower court ruling against a man who was first hired to teach at the University of North Carolina-Wilmington in 1993. He was an atheist at the time of the hire, and subsequently attained associate professor status in 1998. In 2000 he became a Christian, and when in 2006 he was up for consideration for full professor status, the school denied him his promotion because of his Christian beliefs.

So, what should our response be when we suffer persecution? There are several interrelated responses described in Daniel's vision. First, *we must resist the pressure to compromise our faith*: "With flattery he will corrupt those who have violated the covenant, but the people who know their God will firmly resist him" (v. 32). The temptation to compromise morally becomes stronger during periods of persecution. This can be seen in the letter of Hebrews. The historical context of Hebrews—a text that contains some of the strongest warnings in the New Testament against falling away from the faith—is persecution. After recounting the severe persecutions that his readers had suffered because of their faith in Christ in 10:32–34, the author then goes on to warn his audience against falling away from their faith: "So do not throw away your confidence; it will be richly rewarded. You need to persevere" (Heb 10:35–36a). Persecution has the power to weaken our commitment to the faith. But moral compromise must be resisted at all costs.

Second, in the midst of suffering persecution, *we must become encouragers*: "Those who are wise will instruct many" (v. 33a). "Instruct" here does not refer to teaching so much as it refers to encouraging. A close semantic parallel is found in the book of Job. One of Job's friends reminded him, "Think of how you have *instructed* many, how you have strengthened feeble hands. Your words have supported those who stumbled; you have strengthened faltering knees" (Job 4:3–4). The Hebrew word for "instructed" here in Job is the same word used in Daniel 11:33a. Job's words of instruction were of the supportive and strengthening kind; that is to say, Job was known as an encourager. That is how we should respond when persecuted: as encouragers.

Encouragement is probably one of the most underrated gifts of the Holy Spirit. In the spiritual gift list in Romans 12, it is usually overshadowed by some of the more prominent gifts listed there: prophesy, teaching, and leadership, never mind the more eye-catching gifts mentioned in 1 Corinthians 12. And yet, we should never underestimate the value of encouragement. The power of encouragement can be heard in testimonials. Rarely will someone say something like, "I'd like to thank so and so for teaching me about appreciating art" or "for showing me the correct technique for shooting" or "for clarifying the difference between pitch and melody." Far more often, what you will hear is how so and so "inspired me" or "believed in me" or "took me under her wing"—all are code words for encouragement.

There's Hope for the Persecuted

In his book *Spiritual Stamina*, Stuart Briscoe tells the story of something that happened to Howard Hendricks, the renowned Bible professor, Christian educator, author, and influential mentor to many pastors and church leaders. Howard had come from a broken family and was a problem kid. During his first day in fifth grade his teacher said, "Oh, Howard Hendricks. I've heard a lot about you. I understand you are the worst kid in school." That year Howard did whatever he could to prove her right. When the next year rolled around his sixth-grade teacher said to him, "Oh, so you are Howard Hendricks. I've heard you are the worst boy in this school." Hendricks thought, "Here we go again." But then the teacher continued, "And you know what? I don't believe a word of it." And Howard said that year his teacher did everything she could to help him and encourage him and praise his work. She believed in him. Hendricks credited her with changing his life forever.[2] Encouragement can help people accomplish amazing things. I like Christian authors Larry Crabb and Dan Allender's definition of encouragement: "Encouragement is the kind of expression that helps someone want to be a better Christian, even when life is rough."[3] According to the angel's message to Daniel, the wise distinguish themselves by the way they encourage other people.

During the Maccabean Revolt (one of the periods described here by the angel), the Hasidim, a coalition of the pious members of Israel, sought to encourage and rally their fellow Israelites to walk in piety according to the standards set for them in the Mosaic Law, despite intense opposition to their faith. The book of 1 Maccabees, a text addressing Jews in the second century BC, describes events surrounding the Maccabean Revolt. At one point it records how Mattathias (one of the Jewish leaders) was publicly offered silver and gold by the king's officials, if only he would abandon his faith and adopt the way of the Greeks. In front of all of the Israelites who had assembled with him, Mattathias boldly responded,

> Even if all the nations that live under the rule of the king obey him, and have chosen to obey his commandments, every one of them abandoning the religion of their ancestors, I and my sons and my brothers will continue to live by the covenant of our ancestors. Far be it from us to desert the law and the ordinances. We will not obey the king's words by turning aside from our religion to the right hand or to the left. (1 Macc 2:19–22; NRSV)

---

2. Briscoe, *Spiritual Stamina*, 231–32.
3. Crabb and Allender, *Encouragement*, 10.

We've Lost. What Now?

For the author of 1 Maccabees, Mattathias's words simultaneously speak at two different levels. For unbelievers the message is: we will not cower to your pressure to conform us to your way of life. To believers the message is: follow my example of no compromise.

For Christians today, to act wisely in the midst of our social-cultural marginalization means that our messages of renewal and reformation must target not only society but also the church. Churches must never abdicate their prophetic office of calling unbelievers to repentance. However, when we compromise ourselves morally we also compromise our message. Consequently, it falls on hardened hearts. When the Western church experiences renewal—when we start living up to our high calling in Christ—only then will we regain the ears and hearts of our society. Only then will we begin to minister from the margins with power.

Third, *in extreme situations the proper response to persecution may be martyrdom*: "[The wise] will fall by the sword or be burned or captured or plundered" (v. 33b). In some instances, a firm stand for Christ will lead to the death of the witness. It did for Stephen (Acts 7:54–60). It did for James (Acts 12:1–2), as well as the other apostles. A number of years ago Denys Blackmore, the executive director of Every Home for Christ Canada, shared a story at an Ottawa missions rally I attended, about something that had happened in Nigeria only months earlier. A fifteen-year-old Nigerian youth found a gospel tract, read it, believed it, and prayed to receive Christ. Filled with newfound joy, he found his parents and told them what he had done. The father, who was a high-ranking official in their village, became furious and told his son that if he did not renounce Christ he would be executed. The boy's mother pleaded for her son's life and begged the father instead to banish him from the village. But the enraged father rejected her pleas for clemency. After giving his son some time to think about the gravity of his circumstances, the father approached his son and asked him of his decision. The youth knew that Jesus Christ had saved him from his sins and was now living inside him. He could not renounce what he knew in his heart to be the true. So, the father took the boy to the village center and, before the town's people, decapitated his son. Thankfully, it has not gotten that bad in the West. Still, although martyrdom seems like an impossible scenario in Western civilization, consider this: how many things have we witnessed in the last fifty years in our society that previously would have been unthinkable? Who knows? Perhaps in the next fifty years Christian martyrdom will not be so foreign a concept in the West. But even then, God's sweeping control over all earthly affairs can offer us hope in that time.

Finally, when suffering persecution, *we must be committed to walk in an attitude of humble expectation*, since "[s]ome of the wise will stumble, so that they may be refined, purified, and made spotless until the time of the end, for it will still come at the appointed time" (v. 35). We must walk in humility because we are told that it's not just lukewarm, superficial, or backslidden believers who can crack under the pressure of persecution, but sometimes "the wise." Peter, the "Rock," Jesus' lead disciple, triumphantly proclaimed to the Lord that even if every other disciple should fall away during the time of Jesus' persecution, the Rock would never fall away. Well, we all know how that one ended: the Rock crumbled like a cookie under pressure.

What does the text mean here when it speaks of "stumbling"? The word translated "stumble" appears frequently throughout the Old Testament (including six times in the book of Daniel: 11:14, 19, 33, 34, 35, and 41) and typically refers to physically falling, usually in battle. In light of the period of history to which it refers in Daniel (viz., the reign of Antiochus IV), "stumble" here probably refers to the pious Jews who fell in battle. By way of extension, however, the word also connotes spiritual stumbling. Once again, the verses in Job 4 offer us insight: "Think how you [Job] have instructed many, how you have strengthened feeble hands. Your words have supported those who *stumbled*; you have strengthened faltering knees" (vv. 3–4). As far as I can tell, Job was known not for his orthopaedic expertise, but for encouraging people who had stumbled spiritually. Thus "stumbling" can refer to both physical and, perhaps of greater relevance for our day, spiritual stumbling.

The reality is, everyone can potentially stumble. No one is impervious. That is a sobering thought, which should arouse a deep sense of humility. Paul thus warned the church in Corinth, "So, if you think you are standing firm, be careful that you don't fall!" (1 Cor 10:12b). When believers stumble, particularly pastors and leaders, it's all too easy for us to look down on them and consider ourselves morally superior. Sadly, I have been guilty of having this kind of "superiority complex." But it is only by the sovereign grace of God that a believer keeps from stumbling. So rather than feeling morally elite, we ought to feel a deep sense of sadness for that brother or sister who stumbled, and a genuine sense of humility, knowing that "but for the grace of God, there go I."

We've Lost. What Now?

Not only must we walk humbly, but we must also walk with a sense of expectation because God continues to be at work in the wise even when they stumble. The text states that the wise stumble "so that they may be refined, purified and made spotless" (v. 35). Peter said something similar when he wrote that, although Christians may suffer grief in all kinds of trials, "These have come so that the proven genuineness of your faith—of greater worth than gold, which perishes even though refined by fire—may result in praise, glory and honor when Jesus Christ is revealed" (1 Pet 1:7). The refining of our faith involves purging it of impurities that, although they may remain undetected by our sometimes superficial, introspective glances are, under God's perfect eye, exposed as ugly blemishes that can diminish the value of our faith. It is not merely the passing of trials that produces this purging effect, but, I would argue, our failure as well; for it is when we fail that our stains, previously known only to God, become visible to us, prompting within us a deeper yearning for inner change. Therefore, when a brother or sister stumbles, that is not necessarily the end of the story. God will often perfect us through our failure. Therefore, when we fail or we see others fail, we shouldn't assume that that marks the end of the story.

Paul and Barnabas had been close friends and co-ministers of the gospel for years until they parted ways over a bitter dispute involving their junior associate, Mark. Barnabas wanted to take him with them on their next missionary journey, but Paul was dead set against the idea "because [Mark] had deserted them in Pamphylia and not continued with them in the work" (Acts 15:38). Luke never tells us why Mark abandoned Paul and Barnabas in Pamphylia (Acts 13:13), only that Paul felt strongly that Mark should not have. So what happened? "They had such a sharp disagreement that they parted company. Barnabas took Mark and sailed for Cyprus, but Paul chose Silas and . . . went through Syria and Cilicia (Acts 15:39-41). Mark had stumbled earlier in Pamphylia and Paul was finished with him. But that was not the end of Mark's story. Near the end of his life, Paul tells Timothy, "Get Mark and bring him with you, because he is helpful to me in my ministry" (2 Tim 4:11). Since that fateful day in Pamphylia, Mark had matured in his faith such that Paul, now an elder statesman, could consider him to be of great value to him in his final days. Earlier Paul had considered himself finished with Mark. But God was not. As long as God is involved, there will always be more to the story.

There's Hope for the Persecuted

The last part of the angel's message in Daniel 12 points towards the end times. If Daniel thought things were difficult during the reign of the tyrant Antiochus IV (and indeed they were), the angel revealed to him a future that "will be a time of distress such as has not happened from the beginning of nations until then" (12:1a). Unlike his fairly detailed summary of Antiochus's reign, the angel said little about the particulars of this future time of distress (which is probably a good thing), only mentioning that the people of God would ultimately be kept safe: "But at that time your people—everyone whose name is found written in the book—will be delivered" (12:1b). During this awful period, and similar to the time of Antiochus IV, God would continue to sanctify his elect: "Many will be purified, made spotless, and refined" (v. 10a).

Despite the brilliant testimony of God's faithful, we should not expect society at large suddenly to "see the light," for the angel continues, "the wicked will continue to be wicked. None of the wicked will understand" (v. 10b). This moral hardness is the type of response we can expect from our world as we move through the last days. It is in this vain that Paul warned Timothy, "There will be terrible times in the last days. . . . [E]vildoers and impostors will go from bad to worse, deceiving and being deceived" (2 Tim 3:1, 13). If society did not respond favorably to Jesus during the days of his earthly ministry, and if it did not rally around the ministry of the apostles but rather put them to death, then even a church that has been "purified, made spotless, and refined" can surely fair no better. That fact should keep us from formularizing the principles observed in Daniel: i.e., it should keep us from simplistically assuming that if we do A (be like Daniel) then B (worldwide revival) will result. Life is rarely so simple. God and his ways are far too complex to be reduced to an "if A then B" formula.

If that's the case, then what's the point? Why go through all of the trouble and all of the inconvenience of striving to follow in the faithful footsteps of Daniel, if the results cannot be guaranteed? I think there are two answers to this important question. First, at the final judgment God will confer upon his people glory at the great resurrection: "Those who are wise will shine like the brightness of the heavens, and those who lead many to righteousness, like the stars forever and ever" (v. 3). When God judges humanity, the wise will be favorably rewarded: they can expect to share in the bright and shining glory of their God. Certainly the promise of divine reward gave the ever-faithful Paul a tremendous sense of hope and eager expectation: "I have fought the good fight, I have finished the race, I have kept the faith. Now there is in store for me the crown of righteousness, which the Lord, the righteous Judge, will award to me on that day" (2 Tim 4:7–8a). One of the reasons, then, we strive for obedience is that God will eventually reward us.

Second, and perhaps more to the point, is this: because God said so! God created us, sustains us, and has redeemed us through the awesome work of his son Jesus Christ so that we might live the way Jesus lived. Jesus knew that his society would react negatively toward his life and ministry, yet that never deterred him from continuing to live in the faithful the way he did. So too, societal rejection, despite our wise and faithful witness, ought not to deter us from striving to live in a godly manner; hence the angel's final admonishment to Daniel: "As for you, go your way till the end" (v. 13a). The Hebrew word translated "go your way" appears six times in Daniel. It commonly denotes "walk" in the literal sense (e.g., in 3:25 and 4:29). But the word also connotes "walk" in the sense of behavior or lifestyle, similar to Paul's use of the Greek equivalent for "walk" in Galatians 5:16: "But I say, *walk* by the Spirit, and you will not carry out the desire of the flesh" (NASB). The word carries this sense in Daniel 4:37 (to "walk in pride") and 9:10 (to "walk in" or to "keep God's laws"). This is the sense of the word here in 12:13.

Daniel had been given a glimpse into how the end times will be played out. But he was not to waste his time getting caught up in the vain speculation that so often surrounds end-times prophecy discussions. Rather, he was to go his way: to keep living the exemplary life he always had. Daniel had been told that wickedness would hopelessly continue to increase despite God's people being purified and refined by their Redeemer. But rather than give up, Daniel was to go his way. The angel informed him that he would not live to see the very end—the glorious coming of God. But instead of using that as an excuse to opt out of the divine imperative, he was to go his way: to keep walking wisely and faithfully before his God.

Jacob loved Rachel, and because he loved her he was willing to serve her father Laban as shepherd for seven years. When Laban tricked him and gave him Leah instead of Rachel, what was his response? "That's it, Laban, the deal's over. I'm out of here!" Consider this: Jacob performed his shepherding tasks faithfully, despite being subjected to the unjust conditions set by Laban. Jacob later testified:

> I have been with you for twenty years now. Your sheep and goats have not miscarried, nor have I eaten rams from your flocks. I did

not bring you animals torn by wild beasts; I bore the loss myself. And you demanded payment from me for whatever was stolen by day or night. This was my situation: The heat consumed me in the daytime and the cold at night, and sleep fled from my eyes. It was like this for the twenty years I was in your household. I worked for you fourteen years for your two daughters and six years for your flocks, and you changed my wages ten times. [If not for God] you would surely have sent me away empty-handed. (Gen 31:38–42a)

Jacob was not married to Rachel, so, having suffered in this way for seven years, he would have been justified in moving on, especially given how poorly his "boss" dealt with him. But no, Jacob dutifully continued on—he went his way—serving as Laban's shepherd for another seven, long, difficult years in order to win Rachel's hand.

In these last days, we too must "go our way": the way exemplified by Daniel. The way of Daniel is the very way that we must follow if we are to rise above our own social and cultural exile and minister powerfully from the margins of our society. The way of Daniel is the way of knowing and experiencing God's abiding presence. It is the way of humility, commitment, compassion, and excellence. It is the way of uncompromising integrity. The way of Daniel is the way that deeply knows and effectively shares with others the truths about God: his loving, sovereign, and infinite nature, and his powerful yet sometimes mysterious ways.

Questions for Reflection

1. Does God still "manage" nations as closely as he did during the days of the Bible? What are some signs that he does? Are there signs of his handiwork in the governing of our own nation?

2. What are some ways that you have been powerfully encouraged by someone in the past? What are some practical ways that you can encourage others during difficult circumstances?

3. Have you ever experienced abysmal failure in your Christian walk? In what ways did God use that failure to bring about spiritual fruit in your life?

4. Have there been times when you have been hurt, and you responded to the other party in a manner that lacked integrity? Was there any negative fallout because of your response?

5. Are there positive ways that local congregations who find themselves squaring off against their community (e.g., over building plans, or a Christian school) can respond to unfair complaints and criticisms?

Conclusion

With the steady crumbling of Christendom, the Western church now finds itself where Daniel and his compatriots found themselves over two millennia earlier: in social and cultural exile. Our society, as Bryan Stone rightly observes, no longer has a distinctly Christian memory, background, values, or vocabulary. Consequently, the Western church no longer has "home field advantage." But just as the Babylonian exile did not spell the end for Israel, so too our own exilic marginalization does not mean the end of the church. However, for the Western church to bear the abundant fruit God desires in the twenty-first century, we must make a decisive and fundamental shift in our attitude regarding the present status of the church in society: we are a people in *exile*!

In his book *Church after Christendom*, Stuart Murray describes this prerequisite shift in attitude as an "acknowledging."[1] Church leaders, especially, must acknowledge this (not so) new reality of our current social-cultural landscape. Many refuse to concede this, pointing to the increasing number of mega-churches. According to the Hartford Institute for Religion Research, the number of mega-churches (i.e., churches with an average attendance of at least 1,500 people) has quadrupled in the last 20 years to over 1,600 churches. This statistic, however, is misleading. Approximately half of these American mega-churches reside in the South, a.k.a. "the Bible Belt," where the remaining pillars of Christendom have not yet fully given way. Despite some regional "successes," owning up to our overall social-cultural marginalization is, as Murray points out, "a matter of honesty, not defeatism." Not doing so, he insists, will result in "not starting at the right point

---

1. Murray, *Christendom*, 148.

Conclusion

[in our evangelism], so our assumptions will be skewed and our expectations unrealistic."[2]

To witness wisely means we must begin our story in exile. Since society now lacks a distinctly Christian memory, background, values, and vocabulary, we must assume less knowledge of Christianity on the other person's part.[3] Often we share the gospel assuming far more knowledge and familiarity with the Bible and its basic teaching than we should. Assume nothing; explain everything. Better to heed the request of bumbling boss Michael Scott from *The Office*, when his accountant, Oscar, presented him with the year-end expense report: "Why don't you explain this to me like I'm an eight-year-old."[4]

Since our society has lost its taste for Christianity, to witness wisely means that we must expect longer journeys towards receiving the gospel.[5] God can and does at times draw people to faith in Christ quickly. My own conversion as a twelve-year-old took place at the end of a five-day vacation Bible school. I have known people who received Christ the very first time they heard the gospel. But while God can bring people to faith quickly, I believe the new conversion narrative for Western society in the twenty-first century will be long journeys towards faith in Christ. Consider Daniel: We don't know exactly how long it took for Nebuchadnezzar to embrace the God of Israel. From the time of his first encounter with Daniel to the time of his death was approximately forty years. Sometime within that period the king experienced seven years of insanity before turning to God. So, in all likelihood, Nebuchadnezzar's journey towards faith went on for decades. We should expect more of the same, then, as we minister from the margins: longer journeys towards faith in Christ.

If churches begin to locate and position themselves attitudinally on the fringes, then they will avoid the Christendom-instilled posture whereby "our self-image, attitudes, tone of voice and ways of relating will further damage the already tarnished reputation of an institution associated with a fading culture characterized by oppression, moralism, and hypocrisy."[6] In the Introduction I mentioned Tim Tebow. I believe Tebow was viewed as a polarizing sports figure largely because of where he said what he said:

2. Ibid.
3. Ibid., 155.
4. Quoted from DiGiovanni, "Accounting Skills."
5. Ibid., 156.
6. Ibid., 148.

the twenty-first-century marketplace. A couple of generations ago Tebow would have had home field advantage in the marketplace. His comments, while not accepted by all, would have been received by many in that day and tolerated more easily by most within Christendom—what with most of its Christian memory, background, values, and vocabulary still intact. But with home field advantage out the window, Tebow's humble attempts to witness were genuine and sincere, but not wise.

Kurt Warner, the zealous quarterback of the 2002 St. Louis Rams team I had also mentioned in the Introduction, was once asked about Tim Tebow. I guess you could say that Warner was "Tebow" before Tebow: he was very outspoken in his faith, seizing every opportunity to give a shout-out to Jesus, but rubbing many people the wrong way with his Christian rhetoric. According to Dan Bickley's November 2011 column in *The Arizona Republic*, Warner came to see that whenever Christian athletes make such bold, verbal testimonies, "[The audience's] guard goes up, the walls go up, and I came to realize that you have to be more strategic." He admits that he should have toned down the religious rhetoric and let his actions do most of the talking. Notice that Warner does not say that he should have remained completely silent and simply let his actions do all the talking; rather, there needed to be more of a balance to his witness: less words, more works. Warner thus offers this counsel to Tebow: "The greatest impact you can have on people is never what you say, but how you live. When you speak and represent the person of Jesus Christ in all actions of your life, people are drawn to that. You set the standard with your actions. The words can come after that."[7] This principle of our actions preparing and paving the way for our verbal witness is embedded in 1 Peter 3:1–2: "Wives, in the same way submit yourselves to your own husbands so that, if any of them do not believe the word, they may be won over without words by the behavior of their wives, when they see the purity and reverence of your lives." Christian wives are not to take it upon themselves to nag their unbelieving husbands into the kingdom; rather, they are to win them over without words.

Part of what it means to witness wisely to the culture in which we find ourselves firmly entrenched in its margins involves embracing an approach where we first set the standard with our actions. Clearly, this is how exilic Daniel witnessed to his unbelieving society. He lived a life marked by deep humility, an unyielding commitment to God, genuine compassion,

---

7. Bickley, "Kurt Warner to Tim Tebow."

Conclusion

vocational excellence, and unqualified integrity. Daniel's exemplary life, on the one hand, helped to bridge and even to reduce the spiritual distance between his society and his faith. On the other hand, Daniel's skillful lifestyle established the firm foundation upon which his verbal witness could rest and find its support, and through which his message could be better understood by his hearers.

I believe that social-cultural exile is one expression of God's judgment upon the Western church. Yet, in the mysterious sovereign workings of God, in that one act of divine judgment God has, ironically, also provided the means through which we can begin to reach our society more effectively. One of the greatest criticisms leveled against the church by unbelievers is the charge of hypocrisy: we arrogantly claim to be something that we, in reality, are not. Christians rail against immorality but, come to find out, we live immorally (see the litany of scandalized big-name preachers).

While people tend to use the word "hypocrisy" to describe blatant instances of incongruity between our message and our lifestyle, viewed from a different angle—from the perspective of people inside the church—the word becomes "inauthentic." Professing Christians often leave the institutional church because of what they do not see or feel in local churches: authenticity. All too often many Christians would rather keep up appearances—of being a spiritual person with a perfect life—for fear of experiencing condemnation from their brothers and sisters (who "appear" to have it all together themselves). But if we can't be ourselves in the church, then we are in huge trouble. I find that it's this penchant for keeping up appearances that characterizes Facebook. How many Facebook walls are there that put forward the "my life is so great!" image, when you simply know in many instances that's not the case? Authenticity cannot coexist with a hidden commitment to "putting on a face(book)."

I believe that God in his infinite wisdom has been addressing this problem of inauthenticity through our exile. Christendom has—sometimes inadvertently, sometimes intentionally—produced a culture of inauthenticity, erroneously thinking, "Given the central place we occupy in society, the world must not see us as anything other than the church triumphant. We're too big to fail!" Well, *we've lost*. Christendom has crumbled and the church now lives ignominiously in social-cultural exile in the margins of society. So, *what now?* Now we keep it real. Society now sees us as a bunch of "losers," so there really are no appearances for us to keep up. Society has judged us to be losers, and so has consigned us to its margins. There's nothing for us to fake anymore. But life in the margins means that God has once again given us the opportunity to be authentic. When Paul writes, "Brothers, think of what you were when you were called. Not many of you were wise by human standards; not many were influential; not many were of noble birth" (1 Cor 1:26), one inference is that many of the members of the Corinthian church were not considered wise, influential, or upper-class. Indeed, historians have written volumes demonstrating that the majority of first-century Christians were from the lower socioeconomic classes of society. Therefore, putting on a face to attract unbelievers would have made little sense for them as well.

The church is comprised of drastically imperfect people whom God has graciously chosen to transform into the image of his Son Jesus. I believe living life in the margins actually frees us up to be real, to be authentic. In a bygone era when the church was prominent and esteemed in society, churches and Christians might have felt pressure to keep up the appearance of a pristine life. But this pressure no longer exists today because society has kicked us from our social-cultural perch and relegated us to exile. Putting on a face in the fringes is pointless. Thus, from our lowly position, we now are free to be who we really are, warts and all: people who struggle with making regular time for God, who still find it hard to control their temper, who sometimes neglect their family, who still wrestle with forgiving and letting go. The fact that we have struggles actually affirms that we're moving in the right direction. We're just not there yet—something we need to be willing to admit freely to others. To try to broadcast the image of the perfect Christian life—in other words, to fake it—makes a sham of sanctification. We cannot mislead other people into thinking that we are something that God has not yet made us. Far from bringing God glory, pretending to be what we are not—i.e., being inauthentic—dishonors him.

Exile, then, means that we no longer have to present ourselves as having it all together, especially when we know full well that we don't. We can be real with people. It also means that we can allow other people to be themselves, warts and all—to be real with us—and not judge them for it. Thus, through the "defeat" of exile God has tilled the soil of the church to cultivate a new culture of authenticity among his people, for as theologian David Wells writes, "[P]roclamation must arise within the context of *authenticity*."[8] Authenticity will only enhance our ability to minister more effectively from the margins.

8. Wells, *Above All*, 315 (emphasis original).

Conclusion

Daniel's setting is our setting. We occupy the social-cultural margins of our society. Living life in the periphery is the Western church's reality in the twenty-first century. But Daniel's story must also become our story. If the church is to witness wisely and minister powerfully to society, then we must learn the lessons Daniel has to offer. Only when we follow the wise example of his life and his message will we begin to capture the hearts of the people responsible for our exile.

Bibliography

"Air Canada Rewards Execs." *The Hamilton Spectator*, May 28, 2010. Online: http://www.thespec.com/news-story/2100830-air-canada-rewards-execs/.

Bibby, Reginald Wayne. *Restless Gods: The Renaissance of Religion in Canada*. Toronto: Stoddart, 2002.

Bickley, Dan. "Kurt Warner to Tim Tebow: Let Your Actions Be Your Words." *The Arizona Republic*, November 26, 2011. Online: http://archive.azcentral.com/sports/cardinals/articles/2011/11/26/20111126nfl-kurt-warner-tim-tebow-advice.html. Read more: http://archive.azcentral.com/sports/cardinals/articles/2011/11/26/20111126nfl-kurt-warner-tim-tebow-advice.html#ixzz3MEdTHkKb

Briscoe, Stuart. *Spiritual Stamina: Biblical Workouts for a Lasting Faith*. Portland, OR: Multnomah, 1988.

Broad, William J. "Toppling Theories, Scientists Find 6 Slits, Not Big Gash, Sank Titanic." *New York Times*, April 8, 1997. Online: http://www.nytimes.com/1997/04/08/science/toppling-theories-scientists-find-6-slits-not-big-gash-sank-titanic.html.

Brueggemann, Walter. *Cadences of Home: Preaching among Exiles*. Louisville: Westminster John Knox, 1997.

Crabb, Larry, and Dan B. Allender. *Encouragement: The Key to Caring*. Grand Rapids: Zondervan, 1984.

Davies, Linda. "Psychology of Risk, Speculation and Fraud." Online: http://projects.exeter.ac.uk/RDavies/arian/lindaemu.html.

DiGiovanni. Jennifer A. "Accounting Skills: A Lesson from *The Office*." *Career Info Blog*, January 23, 2014. Online: http://www.fortis.edu/blog/online-degrees/accounting-skills-a-lesson-from-the-office/.

Dunnam, Maxie D. *The Workbook on Living as a Christian*. Nashville: Abingdon, 1994.

Jedras, Jeff. "Strahl Needs to Learn that Ethics Is How You Act When No One Is Looking." *National Post*, January 27, 2014. Online: http://fullcomment.nationalpost.com/2014/01/27/jeff-jedras-strahl-needs-to-learn-that-ethics-is-how-you-act-when-no-one-is-looking/.

King, Martin Luther, Jr. "The Three Dimensions of a Complete Life." Delivered at New Covenant Baptist Church, Chicago, Illinois, on April 9, 1967. Online: http://mlk-kpp01.stanford.edu/index.php/encyclopedia/documentsentry/doc_the_three_dimensions_of_a_complete_life/.

Kohn, A. "Why Incentive Plans Cannot Work." *Harvard Business Review*, September 1993. Online: http://hbr.org/1993/09/why-incentive-plans-cannot-work/ar/1.

Bibliography

Lincoln, Abraham. "Proclamation 97 - Appointing a Day of National Humiliation, Fasting, and Prayer." March 30, 1863. The American Presidency Project. Online: http://www.presidency.ucsb.edu/ws/?pid=69891.

Murphy, Rex. "How Trudeau's Trendy 'Pro-Choice' Secularism Became the Left's New Religion." *National Post*, May 24, 2014. Online: http://fullcomment.nationalpost.com/2014/05/24/rex-murphy-how-trudeaus-trendy-pro-choice-secularism-became-the-lefts-new-religion/.

Murray, Stuart. *Church After Christendom*. Milton Keynes, UK: Paternoster, 2005.

Palmer, Sean. "Does Your Congregation Lead with Integrity?" *The Palmer Perspective*, February 2, 2012. Online: http://www.thepalmerperspective.com/2012/02/02/does-your-congregation-lead-with-integrity/.

Project Canada Surveys. "Religion and Spirituality Remain Pervasive: Latest National Survey Findings." Press release, April 8, 2012. Online: http://www.reginaldbibby.com/images/PCS_Release_Religion_Spirituality_Remain_Pervasive_in_Canada_Easter_2012.pdf.

Staton, Knofel. *Heaven-Bound Living: Light for the Journey*. Cincinnati: Standard Publishing, 1989.

Stone, Bryan P. *Evangelism after Christendom: The Theology and Practice of Christian Witness*. Grand Rapids: Brazos, 2007.

Van Gelder, Craig. "Missional Challenge: Understanding the Church in North America." In *Missional Church: A Vision for the Sending of the Church in North America*, edited by Darrell L. Guder. Grand Rapids: Eerdmans, 1998.

Vossoughi, Sohrab. "How to Stand Out? Try Authenticity." *Bloomberg Businessweek*, May 28, 2008. Online: http://www.businessweek.com/stories/2008-5-28/how-to-stand-out-try-authenticitybusinessweek-business-news-stock-market-and-financial-advice.

Wells, David F. *Above All Earthly Pow'rs: Christ in a Postmodern World*. Grand Rapids: Eerdmans, 2005.

"What Is God's Eternity." *Closer to Truth*, season 11, episode 9. Broadcast on PBS. See http://www.closertotruth.com/episodes/what-gods-eternity.

Withrow, Brandon G. "Latest Pew Survey on Religious Literacy." *The Author Blog of Brandon G. Withrow*, September 28, 2013. Online: http://www.brandonwithrow.com/?p=761.

www.ingramcontent.com/pod-product-compliance
Lightning Source LLC
Chambersburg PA
CBHW070908160426
43193CB00011B/1407